RAP
DAD

RAP
DAD

A Story of Family
and the Subculture
That Shaped a Generation

JUAN VIDAL

ATRIA BOOKS

New York   London   Toronto   Sydney   New Delhi

ATRIA
BOOKS

An Imprint of Simon & Schuster, Inc.
1230 Avenue of the Americas
New York, NY 10020

First Atria Books hardcover edition September 2018

ATRIA B O O K S and colophon are trademarks of Simon & Schuster, Inc.

For information about special discounts for bulk purchases, please contact Simon & Schuster Special Sales at 1-866-506-1949 or business@simonandschuster.com.

The Simon & Schuster Speakers Bureau can bring authors to your live event. For more information or to book an event, contact the Simon & Schuster Speakers Bureau at 1-866-248-3049 or visit our website at www.simonspeakers.com.

Manufactured in the United States of America

10 9 8 7 6 5 4 3 2 1

Library of Congress Cataloging-in-Publication Data

Names: Vidal, Juan.
Title: Rap dad : a story of family and the subculture that shaped a
   generation / Juan Vidal.
Description: First Atria Books hardcover edition. | New York : Atria
   Books, 2018. | Description based on print version record and CIP
   data provided by publisher; resource not viewed.
Identifiers: LCCN 2018005010 (print) | LCCN 2018016494 (ebook) |
   ISBN 9781501169410 (Ebook) | ISBN 9781501169397 (hardback) | ISBN
   9781501169403 (tradepaper)
Subjects: LCSH: Vidal, Juan. | Journalists—United States—Biography. |
   Fatherhood—Social aspects—United States. | Colombian
   Americans—Biography. | BISAC: BIOGRAPHY & AUTOBIOGRAPHY /
   Personal Memoirs.
Classification: LCC PN4874.V53 (ebook) | LCC PN4874.V53 A3 2018
   (print) | DDC 070.92—dc23
LC record available at https://lccn.loc.gov/2018005010

ISBN 978-1-5011-6939-7
ISBN 978-1-5011-6941-0 (ebook)

Para mi madre,
María Isabel

"We're human beings, my son, almost birds,
public heroes and secrets."
   —Roberto Bolaño

"I'd like to send a shout to the fathers that didn't raise us."
   —Earl Sweatshirt

"I put it down on paper and then the ghost does
not ache so much."
   —Sandra Cisneros

Part I

Memory Lane

True in the game, as long as blood is blue in my vein . . .

1

WE GREW UNDER THE GRAY of a lingering paranoia. The icebox, like the arms on the rusted swivel chair, needed fixing—the beat-up clock and random knobs on the telly, too. But we stopped sweating it just as quick as we could storm the block with no parentals. I'd read that in old Greece, the children dreamed away in wicker baskets, made games with miniature chariots and fed goats and weasels. At seven they took to primary school, learned Homer and how to play the lyre. How it began was all this. This to become, or to learn to become. Not here. Not for the wild things in the 305 and the 954. Raised by women, we searched for Animal Chin and dug for meaning in the fighting words of Leroy Green and Tito Santana. We did the knowledge, and we tripped over it just the same.

THE EIGHTIES MADE US. They also saw the ascent of crack, neo-expressionism, and what would become the soundtrack to our lives: hip-hop. We were awed by the pedestaled beings on the tube, the def poets in their flawless fits, and the jersey'd watercolor figures leaping high as the sun. MCs, ballplayers, the kung fu man whose family never called him Bruce but "Little Phoenix." Everything they did we tried, eager for someone to emulate. We were the fatherless searching for our footing, steady on the hunt for a narrative. Our mothers carried what seemed like the weight of the world on their backs. They were scrappy, selfless. They loved hard and worked their fingers to the pink. But the void we felt was inescapable. Then it hit us like something furious blazed in from afar. This thing with its beauty, its built-in contradiction. It was loud and savage and free, like us. We were drawn to hip-hop's magnetic pull, transfixed by its starts and stops. Like the Spanish and Patois and Creole of our homes, it became a part of us—it carried the same force as our mother tongues. Only it wasn't in the language of our mothers, so they couldn't teach it, or take it away. They damn sure tried. At Silver Lakes Middle, it was our strut, how we cracked jokes. We invoked KRS and the Jungle Brothers, and in '92 as a nod to Rakim, Gino got "Don't Sweat the Technique" etched in his fade. We lost it, and that chico was king for the whole quarter.

In those days, many of us came to see our fathers as ghosts, apparitions who would appear one moment and be gone the next. They were in love, then they weren't; they played at life. They seldom prospered and never mastered the minutes. There was only that, the days swooping past with the wind in their hair. Over and over they broke our hearts. But we the children ate our fill and grew. Some of us went to war, some to university. Others nowhere fast. We all aged, and many became husbands. Some, fathers. Soon there were lawyers, therapists, preachers, tons of figuring and psychoanalysis. A lot of cheating and come mierda. Regrets, fractured family structures. Everyone trying to manage, never having learned how to properly navigate it all. We were never taught the way of stand-up cats that handled theirs. We had to dig deep, and in time some of those skills came, like the night. Night always came, and that was the truest thing. Right and left, we saw other grown-up kids who were left to chance. The faint memories of distracted fathers.

This is the story of us.

2

WE LIVED IN A BROWN BRICK HOUSE in the southeast part of the sun-shine state, a stone's chuck west of I-95. Nights I could feel the traffic rumble as I dreamt of Third Earth or guarding the Castle Grayskull with a sword. There were three bedrooms, two bath-rooms, and a small den that housed mounds of records and dusty photo albums. My two brothers, Alejandro and Andres, shared a room. Still, they both preferred to nod off in mine, the three of us packed like canned beans on a twin bed that creaked every time we moved. My folks bickered down the hall, their arguments mostly centering on my father's whereabouts—where he'd been all week and why he carried the scent of some other man's wife. Drugs, too. The first time I saw my father do coke I was about six. I'd ambled into the kitchen for bread at some godless hour—my hunger was always fierce and unceasing—Batman Underoos in full effect. I didn't know what the powder was on his stache, but I remember wishing he'd take me to see the snow. I'd seen it some in New York City, where I was born, but palm trees and sprawling beaches had erased those memories. A family vacation that never was is one of my earliest recollections. Less than halfway there my father decided it was enough. My brothers and I sat in the back of our Astro van with the luggage, a cooler, and two fishing poles. He was beat from a night out, but that morning my father said, "You think he's the only one who can take you anywhere? Let's go." He tossed a duffel bag onto the bed and started shoving clothes in it, his and my mother's, whatever was near. "You think that gringo is something grand, don't you? Well, your father is taking you on a trip," he said. "¡Apúrate!"

Weeks before, our neighbor Joe had taken a few of us neighborhood kids to the Florida Keys, some seventy miles south. His son—Joe Junior—was in my grade. Joe Junior, who we called Joey, had the gadgets and a freestyle bike and one of those transistor radios we would have murdered for. We had a few decent trinkets at my crib but Joey, an only child, had a Hot Wheels race track and we would go at it for hours. His mother died in her sleep when he was three, so it was just him and his pops and a yellow-eyed cat called Jesse. The only person I'd ever seen with more hardware than Joey was my primo Juan Carlos. But after Hurricane Andrew tore through his house in Kendall, he lost the bulk of it. My tíos replaced what they could, but his collection was never the same.

Joe was like the stand-in dad for our close-knit squad. Willie's was dead, Doug Oh's worked a ton, and mine was busy hitting skins somewhere. Joe took us fishing and swimming and we did karaoke at some ratchet dive called Woody's in Islamorada. We always came back full and happy, eager to tell our mothers about our adventures:

how many fish we'd caught and how next time, next time for sure, we'd be man enough to bait our own hooks. Those shrimp are just too quick, we'd say. And they bite.

About an hour into the drive to Key Largo, my parents started with the yelling. My father was sucking a beer in the passenger's seat and Ma was at the wheel. She was going on about something, and my father, already in a pissy way, got worked up. He'd been in a bad way since the dry cleaning business folded. And the limo business before that, both of which my grandfather, Ma's father, had owned. We weren't even close to the stretch on Federal, but things felt doomed. Finally, when we were posted at a red light, my father let out an expletive and flung his arms like an umpire. "¡Carajo!" he said, and broke out. The light changed and Ma didn't hesitate; she pumped the gas with cool focus and fury. I turned around and watched as my father, now shirtless, took the last few swigs of his Presidente and chucked it in the bushes. Then he began to fade in the distance, becoming smaller and smaller in my eyes and mind.

If your parents went to war like mine, it was best to grab your board and dip. We'd say, "Freak this," and head for Mr. Bill's, the grocer on Commercial. None of us were allowed to go past the "Woodlands Estates" sign by ourselves, but that didn't keep us from spitting on it as we rolled by. We'd speed down the sidewalk against the traffic that made our boards shake like mini tremors. Once, Doug Oh hit a stone and sent his new Powell-Peralta board onto the road. A semi smashed it in two and parts went flying, like a dream just out of reach. Doug had to walk home carrying both halves, and he struggled to put together a believable story. You can bet he got the belt when his dad came home from work, too. He was always doing something to get the belt. Doug Oh, no board and leather-worn nalgas.

OUR FATHERS were like foreign objects of a kind. Few of them born in the country of their children, their lives were supposed to say something about progress. They mostly did the opposite. Then again, it seemed American to whip your kids with belts when they split their boards or failed to mind their tone. At Mr. Bill's, we'd put candy and pickled sausage in our shorts without paying. Willie always copped a lemonade or ginger ale, and that was like a decoy, as they say. At school I'd sell the sweets I had left over, Blow Pops and Bottle Caps, for whatever I could get. It was all profit, and fools never minded spending the money so long as they got their sugar rush. No bull, I could push packs of Smarties for a buck each and be set for days. That's good business, I'd tell Alejandro back at home. Good, solid business. He always wanted to tag along, but that was a gamble. If I knew there might be potential danger waiting, I'd order him not to follow. Even small mischief like ding dong ditch I tried to keep him from. It felt responsible to set boundaries like that.

Some nights, Ma would be up late, at the kitchen table sewing. The money she earned at the nail salon wasn't much, and she'd stay tinkering with dresses and tops, using what she'd learned in junior college for extra cream. Friends brought her clothes and she'd make the alterations. Sometimes I'd sneak out of bed to watch her as she toiled, her busy hands, her constant yawning. She would sketch and measure, stitch and seam. One night she fell asleep with the machine still clicking and I had to wake her. "I'm up," she said. "Just needed a minute." On the days Ma took her finished work back to the salon, she'd come back with bags of food—steaks and frozen pizzas. "I got your favorite," she'd announce. "Take a look." In that way I figured Mr. Bill and I were straight. I lifted candies, and Ma made it right with bigger purchases. There was a certain joy I got from Ma's victories, her provision and steady grind in the shadow of an absent and unfaithful husband.

He had his women, my father; all kinds of them. Short, tall, dark, fair-skinned, always in shape. Once, he brought me along on a date, if you can believe that. He told Ma he needed to get some items from the market and she insisted he take me with him, because I hadn't been out all day and boys need the air. "It'll be good for him," she told my father. Eventually, he caved. I remember a dingy bar and a thin woman with legs smooth as water. She wore a white skirt that stopped just short of her knees. My father enjoyed the woman's company, which he demonstrated with his hands. "Here's a paper and pen," he said to me. "Make something nice for your mother. Over there," he said, "where the light is good."

MY MOTHER'S LOYALTY to my father not only spoke to her patience and her capacity to forgive, but also her naiveté. She gave and gave. She wanted badly to be seen again, to salvage the union. When my father was hungry, Ma fed him. When he wanted children, she birthed them. In truth, neither one of my parents was free in this cycle, this foolish dance of pleasure seeking and pardoning and rationalizing. Cheating was only the half. In time, there were weeklong binges and violent episodes; there were empty vials left in sinks and shady company parked out front. Back then, it wasn't unheard of for armed men to appear out of department store aisles and vacant lots, looking for my father. Looking for us. At first they seemed like friends and associates, and perhaps at one point they were. They'd greet my father with a handshake, exchange banter, and vanish. But after a while, things turned suspect.

Years later, Ma would share with me a particularly disconcerting story.

Some weekday morning, there was a knock at the door. I'd missed school that day due to some ailment or other, and was curled up under a chair with a pile of Garbage Pail Kids. Ma sighed and answered reluctantly, like she anticipated a stir. Two men were there to greet her. They were looking for my father, naturally, who hadn't been home in days. The men asked Ma what school her boys attended, said they wanted to pay them a visit. She had no answer for them, and they didn't push. No problem, they said, and took off. But they were determined to locate my father, who, as Ma learned, owed them a pretty penny. Ma dug up information, pieced together details, and concluded that my father did not, in fact, manage a hotel; nor was he a bartender; nor did he help run a video store. No, he was dealing in narcotics. And the men who visited our home, she came to know, were tied to the Pereira Cartel, an organized network of ruthless traffickers who would dispose of anyone who dared crossed them. My father's cousin Pinzón was in the business of transporting tons of blow in the fake hulls of speedboats. Fool got smoked in Venezuela years later after a deal gone sour. If my mother had not been acquainted with fear up until then, the visit from these miscreants was its crude introduction. Slowly, she began to formulate an escape plan, taken to the brink by this new and terrifying reality: the man who was once her everything was now endangering everything she lived for.

The next night, while her children slept, Ma was tipped off by a neighbor who'd seen my father with a woman at a nearby filling station. She got jacked way up and put rubber to the road. As she approached the Mobil, Ma saw my father and the woman pulling off. Ma followed closely, but made no effort to remain inconspicuous. When the woman, who was driving one of our vehicles, noticed they had company, she floored it. Determined to not let my father get away without meeting her gaze, Ma gave chase. For almost half an hour, she stalked the yellow glow of his taillights all over the city, her heart pounding as she weaved in and out of traffic, like a madwoman. She knocked over recycling bins, pummeled flower beds. But when reality set in, she cooled down and made her way back home to her boys, who were just as she'd left them. Ma never mentioned the incident to my father, and it's uncertain whether he ever knew who'd pursued him that night.

I KNEW VERY LITTLE about what my father did for work when I was a child. All I knew was that we had a house, clothes, food; and when I needed a new skateboard or dough to sign up for soccer league, I usually got what I asked for. Still, he always seemed to be between jobs. Ma said the reason my father didn't last long in his places of employment was because he always wanted to be the boss.

I should be calling the shots was his sentiment wherever he set foot. He was vocal about it, too. Where sensible people understand the concept of working your way up into a leadership role, my father did not. In all his adult life he would undermine superiors without hesitation, propose better ways of achieving goals. Then when he got canned for overstepping boundaries, he would fail to see the deeper problem.

Another day, I was home sick with a low-grade fever. I'd been left in the care of a family friend so Ma could run a few errands. My plan was to lounge in my pajamas all afternoon, watching television until Alejandro and Andres came home. I was lying on the sofa looking for nudity on HBO when my father bolted in. "Shouldn't you be at work?" the woman asked him. "Don't you worry about that," he said, and made her scram. "Mijo, get up," my father commanded. "Let's go find some trouble." I felt terrible but pushed through my weakness and went to dress. When I returned, I observed through the cracked door as my father pulled a wad of bills from a suitcase. I'd never seen that much cash, and even to my callow mind, it was unsettling. We're rich, I thought to myself. "No, slip on your bathing suit," he instructed as I walked in. "We're going someplace special." I assumed he meant we were headed to West Wind Park, a nearby community center where we would go to swim and ride the swings on weekends. I normally went with Joe and the crew, so I was glad to be trooping it with my father for a change. After we'd been driving for some time, it became clear that I'd assumed wrong. I didn't have the strength to ask where we were going, so I hung tight, growing drowsier by the second. When I woke up an hour later, I was confused. We pulled into a massive park with the biggest water slides I'd ever seen. The slides twisted and turned, they were suspended in the sky beneath hot white clouds. They had names like Brain Drain and Big Thunder. Was I dreaming? "Let's go," my father said, his rough and freckled hand reaching out for mine. The place was every kid's fantasy; there was a wave pool, a lazy river. I'd seen it before in commercials, and the prospect of visiting had, for one reason or another, seemed improbable. Now here I was, and with my pops at that. The best part was, because it was the middle of the week, the lines were either short or nonexistent. We skipped from one ride to the next, cheerful as can be, the sun beating down on us. I couldn't imagine anything better. My parents had been fighting ceaselessly, and this was a welcome respite from the swearing and the accusations. "I'm starved," I said, as we tried to catch our breath after braving the Riptide Raftin'. My father went to fetch food at the snack bar, and I kicked back poolside, people watching in the warm sun. Sitting there, I remembered that I was ill, and I felt tired and frail. I'd pushed my body too hard and was paying for it. I looked over and saw my father conversing with a woman in the line. I figured they knew each other by the way they were cackling, and how he was stroking her shoulder playfully. I didn't make much of it. When he came back, we ate nachos and drank soda by the lazy river.

Only in retrospect can I see that the way my father interacted with random sucias was problematic behavior for a married man. He was always so flirty that I'd grown desensitized to it. Sometimes it was difficult to distinguish friendly chitchat from plain indecency, except for when it was obvious like with that skirt at the bar.

But public pools and beaches were prime locations for my father to spit game. Desperate housewives frolicking around in two-pieces were one of his specialties. Still, afternoons like this were rare in those early years, and I took what I could get. No beef. No curses or dishes being launched across the room. Sure, he brought those things on himself. But it felt good to steal away and just be father and son, lamping on an off day. All of that came crashing down after my father left for the restroom. After he'd been gone several minutes, I decided to go looking for him. When I turned a corner, I saw him necking with the same woman he was rapping to earlier by the snacks. He had her pressed up against a wall, he was kissing her and rubbing her thighs. I ran away, in disgust. On the drive home, there was mostly silence. I told him that I felt nauseous and wanted to shut my eyes. He didn't know I saw him and that bruja sucking the soul out of each other. Even one of our greatest days spent together is tainted with his brute lust.

My father's urges eventually became strongholds, until he couldn't be trusted with his own life, much less a family. It's true that he sacrificed us on the altar of dime pieces, late-night parties, and blow. But I never believed his carelessness was born from a lack of love. Instead, it was symptomatic of addictions that he couldn't easily overcome. He had no more control over his health than a man whose body is ravaged by cancer. I vowed early to never go that route, but who could know. More and more I began to live in my own head. And when the noise became too much, when the wars grew too ugly, I turned to things like martial arts flicks and rap records. Something had to give, and I found a kind of solace in fight scenes and dirty break beats.

It wouldn't be far-fetched to say that hip-hop helped raise me. My favorite albums nurtured and offered perspective during uncertain times. Music in general has that power, certainly, but not with the level of agency that rap does.

On "Keeping It Moving," a cut from A Tribe Called Quest's *Beats, Rhymes and Life*, Q-Tip posits that while valuable, hip-hop can't tell you how to raise a child or treat a wife. And though his logic is not necessarily flawed—we have to be reasonable about what art can truly accomplish—it's not to say rap lyrics can't instruct, enlighten, and, in some cases, save. There have been people who, upon hearing a track at the perfect hour, found the strength to keep living. Although the culture's elements should never be regarded as one's sole means of education, artists have long served as sires and spiritual advisers. Rappers, many of whom were not much older than me and my friends, became the reverberations of father figures. They imparted hard-won lessons not at the dining room table but through cassette tapes and videos. The gems Phife Dawg dropped—juxtaposed with the poetic allure of Q-tip—gave Tribe a gleam; it confirmed everything I felt but didn't have the words for. I was drawn to these and other characters. Their anger, their violence, even the ways in which they publicly processed their own fatherlessness. And I was open, word to Buckshot and Black Moon.

More than anything, I was looking for heroes. I was looking for Joes, but I needed younger ones who could validate my experience and put me on game.

When I first heard Public Enemy—that day the clouds broke open—I knew their influence would be real and lasting. I'd needed a vehicle to help channel years of angst, and *It Takes a Nation of Millions to Hold Us Back* was choice.

We were in detention when I overheard Domingo talking about how he needed a fresh cut. "Can't be busted for this jam, right?" he said to Tomás, to which I replied, "I got you, my man." The plan was I'd take the bus to Domingo's place and shape up his Gumby-style cut out back. Problem was, and I dared not say this to Domingo, I'd never done so much as a fade in my whole life. But I liked to volunteer myself for whatever randomness came my way—indeed, my audacity was remarkable. Domingo had the clippers and a few bucks to spare so reason was clearly on my side.

The first thing I noticed at Domingo's was the pool table. I'd played a few times at Woody's, the dive where my neighbor Joe used to take us, so I talked my smack. Watch, I warned Domingo with the certitude of a pro at billiards. Step and get waxed. He set up the 9-ball and whipped me bad. "Coño, you're rusty as hell." He made sandwiches and blasted tunes, bass coming off the walls like a concert. Then PE came on out of nowhere, and me: "Mingo, what the hell is this?"

"Here the drummer get wicked."

My work on Domingo was decent, a low fade with a clean part down the front. "Tight work," he said, and I nodded. Easy green, hand over fist. Of course, Ma had to leave work to pick me up, an inconvenience that cost me no more than a stern lecture on the ride home. I wish I could say that, while frustrated by my lack of consideration, she commended my drive and entrepreneurial spirit but I can't recall. I didn't hear a word she said the entire drive. My mind was lost in the business of Armageddon and captivated by the visceral power of "Terminator X to the Edge of Panic."

My casual respect for Public Enemy soon turned to admiration. It was more than poetry, menacing drums, and turntablism. This was philosophy and sociology; it sounded like righteous indignation and protest. And I'll be damned if it didn't kiss my soul.

WHEN THEY HOOKED UP with Anthrax in 1991 to reimagine their head banger "Bring the Noise," Public Enemy incited a rap-metal riot in the collective musical consciousness like never before. The song eclipsed the madness of the original and the abrasiveness of the Slayer-sampled "She Watch Channel Zero?!" It blurred the lines of genre and intent; it established the Prophets of Rage as purveyors of something that could endure.

"Soul control, beat is the father of your rock 'n' roll," rapped Chuck D with matchless conviction.

The collaboration signified a step forward not only for Public Enemy, but for pop culture at large. It showed that with the proper moving parts working in a concerted effort, anything was possible. In their joint tour, which featured funk rockers Primus as the opener, Public Enemy and Anthrax were going for the jugular of doubt. That's how Chuck D described it in a 2015 interview at the Rock Hall, in Cleveland, Ohio. He went on to express how intimidated he and his bandmates were in having to measure up to the raw, meteoric energy of their fellow Long Islanders.

"How do you prove yourself with turntables and a unit on stage . . .

you get slaughtered," Chuck D said. "You got to match the intensity not in what they [Anthrax] do; you got to match the intensity in a bunch of different ways that they can't do."

To achieve this, Public Enemy sought to elevate the visual component of their show. They enlisted road crew member Keith Godfrey to learn the ropes from Anthrax light man Rick Downey. This made for friendly competition night after night, as both groups attempted to outdo one another with an electrifying set. It became about who could leave the strongest impression.

I think I understand something of what the self-labeled *rebel without a pause* was getting at, and should like to stretch it further.

My father's days were wasted deceiving his wife and making sporadic jaunts to Colombia, the region of his childhood. He was a man of impulse, my father, the type to fake a heart attack, frighten the kids, and be taken away in an ambulance—simply to gain sympathy from those he hurt. It was pitiful but painfully urgent. I remember accompanying him to Bogotá once, looking out of the bedroom window, twenty-one stories up, listening to the account of how his brother, high on something mind-altering, had leapt, meeting the ground with his face. The way my father told the story was plain as bones, but it had a strange virtue to it.

Through his absence, my father taught me about the beauty of being present. Even when he was around, he was always competing for my affection, and my admiration. It didn't matter whether he was aware of it. My eventual heroes, those I listened to on records and watched on the box, were constantly vying for his spot. And more often than not, their star shined brighter than his.

No other track in recent memory explores the power that we

ascribe to our heroes as deftly as "Pictures on My Wall" by XV. Featured on the Kansas rapper's 2011 mixtape *Zero Heroes*, "Pictures on My Wall" tells the story of a young XV finding his sanity through hip-hop and the posters of the rappers that adorned his bedroom walls.

> *So I put on those headphones and just listened*
> *As the murals on my wall turned to kingdom from a prison*

These mere mortals—Tupac, The Notorious B.I.G., Dr. Dre, Eazy-E—were like gods that hinted at a kind of freedom. They made XV feel like he was a part of something beyond the carousel of his imagination. But his parents couldn't conceive of this, and in the final verse, the disciplinarian of the story storms into XV's room and stands before the altar the boy built for his idols.

> *He starts seeing a bond between me and these pictures*
> *He says, "Look at these niggas, what are they? Father figures?"*

"Pictures on My Wall" is a brutally honest report whose theme will resonate forever and always.

Just as Public Enemy and Anthrax traded blows to win the respect of misfits bleeding themselves in mosh pits, and similar to how my father battled Bruce Lee and De La Soul for my admiration, and the way XV's stepfather couldn't fathom how rap stars could possibly take his place of influence, so it goes for sons and daughters everywhere. Although we go on living as best we can, we're often a product of those who have hurt us most.

BEFORE CHUCK DANGEROUS became Chuck D, he was Carlton Doug-
las Ridenhour. Born in 1960, Carlton grew up amid the tensions
of the Vietnam War and the unrest of the Civil Rights Movement.
Carlton's father, Lorenzo Ridenhour, remembers his son, the oldest
of three, as a quiet kid who gravitated to books. "I used to have to
make him go out to play," he said. "His friends would come walking
all the way over to take him to go play basketball and he would tell
them to go on back."

After graduating from Roosevelt Junior-Senior High School,
Carlton went to Adelphi University. He was into music and
graphic design. While working at the college's radio station, he
produced a promotional piece for the show, called "Public Enemy
No. 1." It made waves and landed on the radar of producer Rick
Rubin, who was instantly sold on the rapper and his dynamic
delivery. It was 1984, and though you wouldn't believe it now,
Chuck D had never wanted to be the front man of an engine for
black resistance. Indeed, he'd wanted to help build the culture, but
preferred to do so from behind the scenes. After some badgering
from Rubin to get serious about a future at Def Jam, Chuck D
agreed. And since his vision was far bigger than just himself,
Chuck D masterminded a music industry assault complete with
all the right bits for worldwide provocation. "It's not Chuck D,
it's Public Enemy," Rubin recalls him saying. There was Professor
Griff, Flavor Flav, Terminator X, Hank Shocklee, The S1Ws, the
whole of it. A crew of militant shape-shifters who could not be

ignored. Rubin was sold; he saw the vision. There was a unit in place, and to him this unit was the definition of counterculture. Public Enemy was the black version of the Clash; pure street, pure punk rock. By 1986, they were set to storm rap with their take on black radicalism.

Public Enemy was an impassioned artistic and social response to the Reagan era. A number of black and Latino families were living well below the poverty line, and getting access to resources became increasingly challenging. People made do with what little they could find, but it was never enough. Unemployment, poor education and health care, dilapidated housing, and the spread of crack cocaine left many desperately scrambling into the underworld, where crime wreaked havoc on any and all. The streets were the battlefield, and the ones in power were supplying every kind of poison to bring about an implosion. The praise Reagan's ideas received from his admirers pointed to a stark cultural disconnect in America. While some have argued for decades that Reagan's epochal presidency ultimately improved America's standing, rappers like Jay-Z ("Blame Reagan for making me into a monster"), Scarface ("Reagan never planned for us to rise"), and Chuck D ("Reagan is bullshit") who experienced its negative effects have long sung a different tune.

Following the success of albums *Yo! Bum Rush the Show* (1987) and *It Takes a Nation of Millions to Hold Us Back* (1988), Chuck D became a father. This is significant because not only was he a mouthpiece for the great rebellion that he helped spark, but now he also had a daughter to look after. And when you're busy forging a cultural institution and educating through rap, which Chuck D called "the CNN of the ghetto," bringing a child into that environment can take the pressure to another stratosphere. But his fire only intensified.

Chuck D impacted so many of us in our formative years. I couldn't articulate it then, but I saw him as a hero, one who disseminated hard truths on the regular. To this day, his effect lingers.

In a November 1990 interview in *Playboy*, Bill Wyman asked Chuck D, somewhat offhandedly, which of his heroes had broken his heart. Chuck D shot back in his wonted candor. "Ralph Abernathy went out like a cold-ass wig," he said, referring to the Civil Rights Movement leader and friend of Martin Luther King Jr., whose controversial book *And the Walls Came Tumbling Down: An Autobiography*, outed Dr. King's alleged infidelities. "It's sad to see people of that stature disappear with no tears," Chuck D said.

BOYS AND GIRLS know only enough about their heroes to want to worship them. They see flesh and bone performing great feats and they cling to the possibility that they, too, might someday do the same. They marvel at the blinding lights, the magic of it all. They see endless glory, and their own outstretched hands. In adulthood, we know the price of putting too much hope in another person. If we're the least bit sensible, we take careful stock of our emotional investments, question everything. We break our own hearts in the process, wondering if we, too, were ever that hero who missed the mark. As a father, mother, friend. And we realize that, yes, we have failed someone. We discover that failure is one of the certainties of life. All of our heroes fall short. They slip through our fingers like so much water. All we can bank on is the cold facts: Three rights make a left, Wu-Tang is for the children. And a hero, like a father, is a thing that you lose. But I wouldn't understand this until much later.

3

DEPENDING ON YOUR PERSPECTIVE, there was a time you might have considered me an outright goon. Not a goon to the level of Bishop from the movie *Juice*, but one with savage tendencies nonetheless. When I was eight, the school principal sent me home for wearing a shirt that read "No Code of Conduct" in bold, black script. Ma's English was shaky then, so its meaning was missed by her. I can't say I fully understood its message either, but you wouldn't have known it by the way the shirt corresponded to my general posture.

I was drawn to the counterculture. Music and art and skateboarding made me want to live louder, turn my life up for the world. Often that meant exposing my ignorance in the process. Like the single time I sported denim backwards because Kris Kross made it seem fresh for a stint. It wasn't, and I got clowned. When you're young, it's permissible to have these gaps in your logic, to act out and never bug over potential repercussions. Everything is about the moment, and how to squeeze more out of it for its own sake. One more swig of the Cuervo; a last hit of the blunt; a bike to jack because I need a ride home and that red Mongoose looks like it flies.

WEEKS BEFORE MY PARENTS' MARRIAGE officially dissolved, my father showed up with a gang of bullet holes in Ma's Accord. That was it. There was no more hanging on to blind hope, or attempting to make excuses for his behavior. Ma knew it, everybody knew it. My grandfather could have killed the man, and maybe I would have forgiven him if he had.

After they split, my father shoved off to the motherland. By now he was on the run—from his enemies and from the law—and had to leave the United States permanently. Ma lost the house and we moved into a small, two-bedroom apartment in Fort Lauderdale. Our first day there, I was blown away by the large community pool and half-court basketball setup. What seemed like dozens of kids my age roamed freely about the complex, on BMX bikes and scooters. Many of them were first-generation Americans like me and my brothers. Their parents were from Haiti, Brazil, the Dominican Republic. Some worked construction, others in restaurants or the night shift buffing floors at the local hospital. Our building sat just behind the school I was to attend for my last couple years of elementary. "Here we will build a home," Ma said. "Just the four of us." The next day Ma took the belt to my ass after she found out I'd sprayed shaving cream all over the exercise equipment in our new gym.

Now I had no choice but to share a room. To save space, Ma found a triple bunk bed on the cheap. I was on top, Alejandro in the middle, and Andres on the pull-out with the built-in drawers.

Sometimes Andres slept in Ma's room, like a sweet, protective boyfriend. He was just a few years old, but he made a ritual of checking the windows and making sure the doors were secured at night. Time passed and not much changed. The three of us boys still stayed up late sipping sugary drinks and feasting on questionable television. When my brothers fell asleep, I'd sneak out to the living room to watch *Def Comedy Jam* and *Spic-O-Rama* in the dark. I'd found a hero in John Leguizamo, whose rage and distrust of authority mirrored my own. While I generally loved my Latin culture—from our food to our music and celebrations—I wasn't always self-assured enough to embrace certain aspects publicly. I hated to stand out when I was younger, unless it was for some commendable deed I'd performed. Nothing bugged me more than when Ma spoke Spanish in front of my boys, even though most of them came from Spanish-speaking homes, too. It wasn't until I saw Leguizamo's one-man show that I came to fully own my identity. I realized that my first language was inextricable from who I was and how I should perceive my place in the world. Anything less was self-hate.

Anyhow, me and my brothers never talked about our father. They were too young to comprehend everything I'd seen. As far as I knew, they were never brought along on dates with side pieces. They didn't watch our father get blitzed in the kitchen or witness his longtime friends turn homicidal. These were my secrets to own and interpret however I chose.

SOON, Ma began taking on more hours at the nail salon. With my father ghost and contributing nothing monetarily or otherwise, the pressure to earn more money grew heavy. Her tips went to food and utilities, her meager paychecks to everything else. There were times she would mail the check for the car note or the phone bill and purposely leave off her signature. The check would get sent back a week later with a reminder to sign and return, which bought Ma extra time to get her paper together. She couldn't afford to pay a sitter when she upped her hours, so Ma now had to take us to work with her two nights a week. She'd pick us up from school and drag us to the salon; a client would wait as Ma got us settled in the back. For the next four hours or so, we'd yell obscenities, get into fistfights, ruin homework, and make it almost impossible for Ma to work uninterrupted. One night, after he'd scribbled over someone's class project in permanent marker, Andres bolted onto the main floor, blood dripping from his mouth. The women looked on, their eyes wide with shock. Ma lost her cool and time suddenly moved slower. Point is, we could be terrible then, and I recall many bloody nights and total pandemonium. "Where is their father?" I heard a bemused client ask once in a voice just above a whisper. Long gone, I thought. Long gone.

My father was born in 1953 in the town of Moniquirá, about ninety miles north of Bogotá. The second oldest of six children, he lived with the burden of birth order on his shoulders. He and his older brother, like many older siblings, were strongly urged to look after the others—and mandated to throw fists when necessary, at school, or the yard. Petty disagreements often came to blows, and their skin grew thicker by the grade. For them, everything came second to preserving their name. Had they let someone slide for disrespecting a Vidal, it might have been perceived as charity, and so they took no shorts. They would never know any other way.

Nestled in the province of Ricaurte in the department of Boyacá, Moniquirá is surrounded by rivers, hills, and coffee plants, its fertile lands producing many natural resources. Bocadillo, a Colombian confectionery made with guava pulp and panela and wrapped in leaf packaging, is among its most well-known exports. My father's father worked in the fields until he moved the family to Bogotá in search of opportunity.

Bogotá in the 1950s could be described as idyllic, depending on whom you ask. People might speak of the extravagant parties and dances and the magic of youth. Perhaps they would tell of their long treks around lush valleys and their weekends spent at a relative's finca up in the mountains. But between 1948 and 1958, hundreds of thousands were murdered in the partisan warfare that came to be known as "La Violencia." My father, and my mother, who was raised to the south, in Santiago de Cali, were bombarded by the daily reports of bloodshed around the country. Though censorship from the government did what it does, and though the threats against journalists and news organizations became heightened during that period, there was no way to ignore what was happening—the chatter in the streets, the paranoia of schoolteachers who had loved ones on the outskirts of the city. But violence has seen varying levels of intensity in Colombia. More than fifty thousand lost their lives in the Drug Wars of the 1980s, during the reign of Pablo Escobar, and in the guerrilla warfare of the 1990s.

FOR MY FATHER, with time and age came anger. And many of his experiences helped breed a deep distrust in the law. Though he may have been a merciless shield for his brothers and sisters, it didn't compare to how frantically my father protected his mother. When he was seventeen, he served his first bid in jail following an altercation. One afternoon, when he and his mother were coming back from the market, a man in his thirties directed a sly comment at my grandmother. My father, barely out of high school, confronted the stranger and demanded he retract his words. When he did not concede, my father saw red and beat the man stupid in the street, nearly killing him. The police came and they put my father away for two months. They said he was crazy.

While my father sat in lockup with slabs of torn flesh under his fingernails, Ma, three years his junior, excelled at Colegio María Auxiliadora, a private Catholic school for girls in the Valle del Cauca. The middle child in a family of five children, she was beautiful and studious. Tall and thin with big brown eyes. As a teen, my mother made grown men stop mid-conversation. But it hadn't always been so. My mother was such an ugly baby that her parents, wonderful as they were, hid her for the first year of her life. When friends tried to make plans to visit, my grandparents would find a way to evade their requests. *The baby is very sick; the baby is sleeping.* Their list of excuses piled up until they finally deemed it safe to parade my mother around like they'd done the others. By the time anyone saw her outside of her immediate family, my mother was already walking and showing off teeth.

As the years went by, my father would demonstrate his contempt for superiors and the simple functions of responsibility. He was bright and warmhearted at the core, but he was also a menace. He scolded well-meaning administrators, defied every order. It seemed jail had changed him for the worse. Instead of accepting those months behind bars as a wake-up call, he dwelled on the sweet reward that was exerting control over another's body if they deserved it. He'd tasted the essence of supreme power, and he concluded that it was good.

NEVER MIND the agony inflicted; never mind the emotional scars that poor bastard would have to endure long after his bandages were removed.

Never mind the violence that reminded onlookers of the civil war in which their country was entrenched.

Never mind that parents and their small children were made to gaze upon a madman who equated justice with suffering.

Never mind the warm sun and the breeze that earlier that day had signaled to all the makings of a perfect afternoon.

MY FATHER'S CONTEMPT for authority got passed down to me, like a piece of jewelry I didn't ask for. In time, I made a sport out of testing the olds. Teachers, guidance counselors, school security guards. Most got the gas face from jump. I didn't thrive on their instruction; I seldom trusted their judgment and I questioned their intentions at a fundamental level. Where this suspicion came from wasn't always clear. But part of it, no doubt, came from witnessing plenty of scum take advantage of their high positions. They were the broken pieces to a power structure we did our best to resist. Basketball coaches were the occasional exception, but they weren't immune to our contempt either. If they said to go right, I might still break left, through the legs and behind the back. My boy Carpio, in an organized city league game one summer, snuffed a kid clean in the jaw for scuffing his Spike Lee Jordans. He got ejected and had to sit out the next game. It would have been easy to defend Carpio's right hook had the two not been teammates. Homeboy was a damn savage.

AT SILVER LAKES, I was a lost one on an uncertain path to middle adolescence. No purpose, no plans. The only things we chased were girls, ill beats, and cannabis, which we got for the low from the Haitians on 10th Court. We filled our days with violence and whatever mischief we could find. We lifted from convenience stores like I'd done as a kid and picked fights with derelicts from other blocks. We bled; we pounded the pavement. When the summer temperatures cooked us like carne asada, we took to the Boys Club, with our raps and our sticky weed. It wasn't long before I started slanging. I reached out to Carpio, who was the plug, and asked him to help me get rich. He mapped out some territory, and soon I was flipping nickel and dime sacks by the racquetball courts. I listened to Onyx and scribbled lyrics of my own invention on scraps of loose leaf as I waited for the burnouts to show up with cash. Admittedly, I was a horrible drug dealer. Nobody taught me how to not be careless with money and I could never save up. It was all dollar slices, movie tickets, and cassette singles. My only real currency was my friends, who I'd have died for if it came down to it. Although we showed love and cherished our brotherhood, we never fully realized just how dependent we were on one another. We rolled in packs of threes or more, at the ready for anything. We organized cyphers, slap boxed outside the bodega. We spent hours unpacking the gems of that day's *Rap City*, who wore what and who unleashed the phattest 16s. Together, we represented power in numbers. We were rappers, poets, skaters, dope pushers, misfits, and sneaker heads; all attention-starved. Our lives revolved around hip-hop and what the music had helped birth in us: an appetite for more, more, more. I grew up with a hunger so big I thought of nothing else. Hunger for food, yes, but mainly for significance. Hunger for meaning. I looked for signs in everything; the nugget of truth in the dirty joke, the broader message in the freestyle. When an older boy, bent on proving his grit, put a knife to my neck at a bowling alley, I wondered if there wasn't something more at play. Was this yet another sign that I was destined for jail or an early grave? I was, after all, my father's son.

I'm not sure why, but to this day I have a fear that I will someday end up in prison. I don't break the law; I pay my taxes. And yet, there's this nagging fear that prison—and I realize the absurdity of this fear—will simply *happen* to me, regardless of my attempts to live well and right.

Anyway. Hard as Ma tried, she couldn't get through to me back when. I gleaned what I could from those not much older, those heroes who, though not fully formed, seemed to occupy thrones and preside over planets. No one then epitomized the contrarian spirit better than the rappers and skateboarders we idolized.

IN THE EIGHTIES AND NINETIES, skateboarding and hip-hop were the most natural of marriages. In their own way, each provided a kind of escape from the world we saw crumbling around us. Fathers went missing and mothers strove to keep their homes intact. Us kids, we went Casper, too, only on four wheels. We were aimless but we were free. And freedom was our faces to the wind.

My first board was the Marty Jimenez Jinx deck with the bat design and hot pink grip tape. It was damn beautiful and, for a while at least, I guarded the thing with all of my might. That is, until I got lazy and thought I could leave it outside the front door overnight. Someone caught me slipping and the goods were his for the taking. Thinking back, I can respect it to a degree. As much as it angered me then, and forasmuch as I'd wanted to punish the culprit, I knew better than to slip like that. I didn't even deserve it if it could be taken from me that easily.

Skateboarding and hip-hop are institutions that, at a point in their respective histories (they've since been more heavily commercialized), spoke directly to the rebel soul of youth culture. They questioned systems, they asked the why of things, they railed against popular opinion. They encouraged individuality and valued personal expression. For those who felt shunned by society or by their parents and needed an outlet, these institutions were there. Skaters were the rejected geniuses who made a playground of the earth around them. They manipulated surfaces to serve their own needs. Groups like The Pharcyde, Freestyle Fellowship, and the Beastie Boys helped define an entire era of hip-hop. They provided the soundtrack to the streets. *Concrete Jungle*, a 2009 documentary by Eli Gesner, encapsulates how both art forms helped inform each other—and how each went on to influence the masses in ways no one could have imagined.

The best track ever to center on skateboarding is Lupe Fiasco's 2006 breakout "Kick, Push." Essentially a love song, "Kick, Push" focuses on the oddballs who found their freedom in skating and in one another. It's the classic scenario: boy meets girl, they hit it off, girl leads boy to secret skate spot, cops shut it down. But even though cops ruin almost everything, the single, and the video, brought Lupe's distinct perspective to the forefront. "Kick, Push" instantly became an anthem, a rallying cry for skaters and a certain breed of rap head. But Lupe made it known early that he never wanted to be seen as a face for the sport. He wasn't rap game Lance Mountain speaking for a subculture. For him, "Kick, Push" was about exploring the relationship between hip-hop and skate culture, and the sense of community they foster when the two coexist. Embracing the power of juxtaposition has always been at the root of Lupe's oeuvre. But his star status has often seemed at odds with what he was taught to value as a boy growing up in Chicago.

In "Hurt Me Soul," another number featured on his debut album *Food & Liquor*, Lupe, born Wasalu Muhammad Jaco, addresses some of this tension and the conflicted feelings he once had toward rap. Because he was taught to value women and girls, he took issue with some of the first records he was exposed to.

Now I ain't trying to be the greatest
I used to hate hip-hop, yup, because the women degraded

As an artist, Lupe has always existed between two worlds: the sacred and the profane. "I grew up juxtaposed," he once told *Entertainment Weekly*. "On the doorknob outside of our apartment, there was blood from some guy who got shot; but inside, there was *National Geographic* magazines and encyclopedias and a little library."

IN MY YOUTH, I'd have related to this idea of juxtaposition, but somewhat in the reverse. Inside there was chaos and enmity. But outside, while there were side-eyes and stickup kids waiting to pull your card, there was also a world that felt beautiful and endless. There were other blocks in other cities in different states. And though I couldn't touch them just yet, I took heart knowing they existed, and that someday I might set foot on them. Perhaps that small sense of hope sprung from lessons I was taught in Sunday school, the few times we attended. Though we didn't grow up in what you might call a religious setting, Ma would tell you that ours was a Catholic home. Una casa Católica. She would make the sign of the cross over us before we set out for the world each day. But in ways, that's where young Lupe's path and mine would cease to converge. Lupe's conviction calls back to his upbringing as a devout Muslim, and as the son of a Black Panther. Both of his parents saw to it that, no matter how harrowing the world was outside, there was always balance.

Before Lupe's father passed away in 2007, he extended just one charge to his son, which he spoke to Lupe's sister Ayesha. In a conversation with Cornel West at Calvin College's 2009 Festival of Faith & Music, Lupe shared this charge.

"Tell Wasalu to tell the truth," his father said. And then he died.

The truth: it's what my friends and I were searching for in our brazenness, and in our misplaced rage. It's what our mothers wanted us to encounter before it was too late, before violence and bitterness grew in us like a virus. When Lupe talks about living on the fringes, and when he rhymes about the teens kicking and pushing in pursuit of something real, it all rings true inside me.

For my father, though, the idea of truth, and what it means to be invigorated by it, existed merely in the abstract. From the time he was young, ducking bullets—both real and figurative—became the norm. And manipulation was his tool. My father bent reality like that supervillain Mad Jim Jaspers. You might say it was passed down from his own father, whose penchant for deception saw no end. He was a creature of the bottle. My grandfather started his days with a tinto at sunrise and slowly worked his way up to the harder stuff, which he slammed back periodically until sleep. He lied, verbally abused his wife, neglected his kids. He didn't model truth to his sons and daughters, like my father didn't model truth to me and my brothers.

As junior high progressed, our circle grew smaller. People began to drift, relocate to other districts. Some got shipped to their parents' country as a form of rehabilitation. Ma always made threats, but I never believed she would follow through. You'll never, I said, after I'd gotten bagged for doing graffiti not far from our house. Domingo was with me, but the cops let him go since it was me they'd caught with the spray can.

I ALMOST ALWAYS made low marks in school, beginning around the sixth grade. One excuse was that the majority of my instructors rarely made the material compelling enough to keep me engaged. Again, Ma spoke very little English during these years, so the help I got at home was limited. The same was true for many of my friends who lived in homes where English was the second language. Even as our folks prized education and admonished us about its value, this was just a fact of life. We were mostly on our own. Few of us got any extra aid in our studies, whether from parents who were too busy keeping us alive or tutors who charged by the hour. Having a tutor was a privilege that not many people I knew had.

Things at school got progressively worse. Ma was getting summoned for parent-teacher conferences every couple months. I was either fighting, flipping off teachers, or napping through their lessons. And even though my spelling and vocabulary skills were on point—Ma loved to brag about my way with words—she knew something had to be done. In the middle of my seventh-grade year, the assistant principal was called upon to intervene. It was usually just Ma and a crabby old woman with horn-rimmed glasses, but this time it was more grave. As soon as Ma walked into the room, she could tell something was different.

"Hello, Ms. Vidal. I'm Mr. Albert."

"How are you? Yes."

"Good, Ms. Vidal, but we're concerned about Juan."

"Yes, yes. I very concerned."

"He just can't seem to stay on top of his studies. He's a smart boy, but he seems to be showing very little effort."

"Yes, it's true."

"Ms. Vidal, have you heard of attention deficit hyperactivity disorder?"

Ma freaked. You'd have thought Mr. Albert had told her I'd contracted some rare and incurable blood disease. Not to mention, Mr. Albert's heavy Creole accent made matters seem all the worse.

"Oh my God! Is he sick?"

"No, no. Ms. Vidal, it's OK. Attention deficit hyperactivity disorder is actually fairly common."

"OK. OK. What do we do? Please tell me what do we do."

"We, Juan's teachers and I . . . well, we think he should be tested. This will help us determine next steps to ensure that your son succeeds academically going forward."

ADHD cases climbed like mad in the late eighties and early 1990s. All across the country, rowdy teens were being tested routinely on the recommendation of agitated teachers and administrators. Doctors were diagnosing kids without blinking. Spacing out in class? Must be ADHD. Constant scrapping and undermining of those in command? It's probably ADHD. Depressed? Sounds like ADHD to us. It was never the teachers and their lack of creativity that were the issue. According to them, it was the fault of the hormone-crazed students who believed they had better things to do than squeeze into a musky portable classroom and be fed half-truths.

A WEEK AFTER THE CONFERENCE, me and Ma sat in a cheerless doctor's office waiting to be called in so I could take my Psychological Assessment. They asked Ma to come back in a few hours since the examination was going to take time to complete. The doctor hit me with mad questions out the gate, asking about everything from my relationship with my parents to my thoughts on life and my supposed inability to concentrate in Math. As he talked, I found myself trailing off, distracted by a number of things. To start, his mustache made him look like a square and sad sexual deviant. There were drab paintings on the walls—dolphins and badly drawn whales—and a candy bowl without any candy. Soon, I called bull on the whole thing.

"Juan, have you heard of attention deficit hyperactivity disorder?"

"Have you heard of Wu-Tang?"

"Yes. Do you like Wu-Tang?"

This instantly bothered me.

Not anymore, I said.

"What else do you like?"

With that, I decided to probe and test his knowledge of Shaolin's finest.

"Ah, doctor, you know, the usual: 'Runnin' up in gates, and doin' hits for high stakes / Makin' my way on fire escapes.'"

"Really? Can you tell me more about yourself?"

"'I was a man with a dream with plans to make cream / Which failed; I went to jail at the age of fifteen.'"

He finally caught on.

"Oh, these are song lyrics?"

"You said you knew the Wu, right? Well, I'm quoting 'C.R.E.A.M.' and you don't know what's what."

"My apologies, I don't know what a Wu-Tang is. Juan, let's talk about school."

He'd already lost my respect, and I saw no reason to give anything else he said much credence.

When Ma returned, I was in the hall, ready to jet. She went inside to settle things with the doctor, and when she came back out, she seemed irked. She handed the woman at the desk a check and scheduled another visit for the following week. The next meeting was more of the same. The doctor went on and on and I quoted Fat Joe and Queen Latifah. Eventually, he saw that he was getting nowhere with me. As we were leaving, he offered a sincere goodbye, probably confident that he would never see me again. I channeled Montoya Santana from the movie *American Me*.

I said:

"You know, a long time ago, two best homeboys, two kids, were thrown into juvie. They were scared, and they thought they had to do something to prove themselves. And they did what they had to do. They thought they were doing it to gain respect for their people, to show the world that no one could take their class from them. No one had to take it from us, ese. Whatever we had . . . we gave it away. Take care of yourself, carnal."

Ma elbowed me in the ribs and the man stared into me blankly.

On the way home, Ma explained that because her insurance didn't cover the full amount of the doctor visits, she had to come out of pocket for $600. She barely had that in her bank account, she said, and the rent was due. I was regretful for having made a joke of the whole mess. "I did this for you," she said. "But you know I can't afford this." She told me they'd prescribed some drug called Ritalin, which, according to them, would help me focus and fight off distractions. Ma told them she would be in touch, but she had no intention of giving me drugs. She'd researched it and heard stories about the side effects of the medication—vision problems, insomnia—and decided to hold back.

"I'm not going to give my baby any damn pills," she said. After that declaration, I never heard another word about ADHD or pills again.

I MADE ENEMIES in those days. I could be cold and sharp-tongued, but I told myself it was mostly for survival. After Ma and Joe—yes, that Joe—had been dating for some time, we all moved in together. Soon they decided to pull Joey out of private school and have him join me at Silver Lakes. Joey was whip smart and athletic, and the Puerto Rican dimes couldn't get enough of his spikey blond hair. They'd point and gawk and he'd turn red. At first, people would refer to Joey as "Juan's White Brother," but that stopped once he flexed his quarterbacking skills on Field Day. One of the few white boys on the intramural team, Joey was beastly when he snapped back to pass. Nobody was nicer. Before long, he had a rep, and he'd sometimes get asked to things I knew nothing about. Though we were as tight as brothers could be, in time we ran with different crews.

Toward the middle of the school year, Joey got invited to a party he wanted to go to and asked me to roll. I had my reservations. Life had taught me to be selective about the places I went without proper backup. None of my boys were going, and a jam with an unfamiliar crowd, in my view, called for more support. At the same time, I didn't want Joey to go alone. The day before the party, I still hadn't made my decision. "Well?" Joey shot during dinner. Ma broke the silence, promising that if I went with him, she'd cop me some new gear for the occasion. That was the end of the matter. An hour later, I was at the mall getting laced with denim and a Georgetown Hoyas T-shirt and matching Starter hat. As we approached the mall's exit across from the Chinese spot, I saw a familiar face grilling me hard; it was a short and stocky Filipino kid who went to my school but was one grade above. He was standing around with his swarm of eighth graders. When me and Ma got closer, suddenly they were all staring me down. I didn't know why. I knew they weren't going to initiate a scuffle then and there, but I was prepared, my fist cocked at my side. The hate in their eyes seemed strange and unwarranted. In the car, I racked my brain trying to recall if I'd flapped my gums at anyone different that week. Nothing stood out.

The party was at the clubhouse of a development called Heathgate. I knew the area well but I never had much reason to visit, not until now. Ma dropped us off and Joey and I made our way inside. My Hoyas fit was fire and I felt fresh and clean. The music was pumping; there were strobe lights, streamers, and tables with an assortment of fare and refreshments. Boys and girls played the wall with their cliques. I thought, *This isn't so bad*. At the least,

I got some new digs just for stepping up. The DJ played decent mixes, and soon I built up the courage to hit the dance floor. There were girls from wall to wall. Later, when I was cooling down by the spread of cold cuts and soda, I caught a few boys eyeing me. At first, I didn't make much of it. I soon realized it was the same crew I'd seen the day before, outside the Panda Express. Then the Filipino kid came into focus and I was seized with regret. I knew this had been a bad idea. We needed to leave, and swiftly. I walked over to Joey, who was talking to the DJ, and told him it was time. "Trust me," I said. "Just c'mon." Joey knew this wasn't a drill, and he followed my lead without hesitation. I didn't want to seem frightened, so we moved toward the door casually. The kids noticed that we were jetting and they gathered like moths to the flame. Everyone else was grooving, not a gripe in the world. Me and Joey speed-walked down the street in the direction of a nearby shopping plaza. I turned around and saw the boys in pursuit. There were six of them. We didn't run; they didn't run.

"Who are those guys?" Joey asked.

"I have no idea."

"Why are they following us?"

"I have no idea."

While I didn't know much, it was clear that their intent was to stomp me out.

By the time we reached the plaza, we'd lost them. We snaked into a department store and disappeared through the back, where we climbed a wall that led into an adjacent neighborhood. When it was safe, we called Ma from a pay phone and she scooped us up. We never mentioned it again, and I never made the same mistake twice. Trouble seemed to always find me, even when I wasn't looking for it. Sometimes I came out unscathed, and other times I wasn't so lucky. But there was always a lesson; I just had to trust the voice in my head.

BY EIGHTH GRADE, Domingo, Tomás, and I had become inseparable. Tomás would boost liquor from his mom's boyfriend and we'd hop on the bus for God knows where. The local bus was a gift for that season of our youth. As a practical measure, sure, but also as a window into human behavior. I saw it all on the number 52: violence, intercourse, every drug imaginable. Most people kept to their books or tunes, but others were far less reserved, mumbling to themselves or feuding with their lovers. The occasional brawl landed a little too close for comfort, but it was all telling. And while I stupidly got lost on a few occasions—I took the bus alone from time to time—I always had my Walkman. I learned to appreciate Dr. Dre's *The Chronic* for the masterpiece it is while adrift in the middle of downtown Miami.

The cyphers we'd hold in the back row are some of my fondest memories of riding public transit as a teenager. It went like this: Domingo would kick the beatbox and Tomás and I would take turns coming off the top or reciting lines we'd penned earlier. We'd wax poetic about each other's mom, bust on a stranger's off-brand shoes, and go into long tangents about how our skill was superior. I tapped into something valuable on those rides. For the first time in my life I came to see my voice as a kind of weapon, the most effective instrument at my disposal. I used it to dazzle my small audience with epic roasts and wisecracks about whatever came to mind. It was a remarkable thing to learn, even as I couldn't fully know the doors it would open later.

THE LAST SUMMER before high school would begin, Domingo perfected his blunt rolling technique and Tomás got a job stocking shelves at Publix. I filled entire notebooks with lyrics and got away with more than I could hope to remember. Before I was fifteen, I'd been jumped twice and arrested three times; petty theft and vandalism. After that final arrest, the one for tagging, Ma's patience was spent. She drove to the station in tears. The night before, she'd found a nickel bag in my wallet, so this was the start of my ending. She'd made a decision in her mind, another thing I wouldn't know until later. On our way back home from the station, Ma told me the arresting officer, something Gugliotta, had said I was a *good for nothing little spic* and was headed nowhere. Naturally, Ma told him off. She'd defended me in principle, but I knew things had to change. I knew that if the officer, who supposedly represented some idea of honor and morality, felt this way, I should take heed. A month later, Ma came upon an article in the *Sun-Sentinel*. The same officer, Gugliotta, had been charged with two counts of burglary. Cops ain't worth a damn, I thought to myself.

We were blazed on some North Lauderdale bud when Domingo said, "Look." He took to the coffee table, corn chips snapping under his feet. Some of our boys were in third period by now and we laughed, pitied them in their lockdown. It was the year *Black Sunday* dropped and the Hill was showing out. "I Wanna Get High" rattled trunks all across a scorching Miami and shook our core type heavy. Compulsive truants, we'd ditched class that day to sing their praises, B-Real and Sen Dog's raps emanating from our bodies like a spell.

"Look," Domingo said, standing on his mother's furniture. "It's no secret that you're all in need of something meaningful to believe in. I mean, really believe in," he said. "It goes like this around these parts. You got it all. You'd think, what with your sunny beaches, your platinum and endless gold, your drive-thrus and stocked mini-marts, you'd be satisfied. Wrong. All this and you've fallen to boredom, toking all day and yearning for something lasting; a well-paved road," he said, "a narrow path. More sex, more noise. Less of you people, though. You damn degenerates with your fast and random ways. As your leader, I've come to understand this," Domingo said, "that perhaps we've been going about this all wrong. Forgive me," he said. "What might be necessary is a fresh cause. A thing without the pitfalls of institutional belief," said the ex-churchboy. "You know what I'm talking about. What we need, I've come to accept, is a new religion. Yes, gentlemen, lend an ear. One with better music, see, more beats; more electric guitar, maybe, more oboe. One for which our devotion might be better understood, shared by every heathen with a heartbeat. See what I'm getting at? Let's shake things up. I'm hinting at a place. Some place where you would not be scorned when politely requesting a second fix of that delicious communion bread. Sound good to you fools? I'm talking merchandising efforts that dazzle, campaigns that tug at the core. We for something raw and revolutionary, something for us, who are far from prophets but evangelists of a new day. Talk to me. I'm preaching up in here and I think you love it." We said, "Chill," but he didn't let up. "You love it."

"We bear witness, we picket," he said. "We stumble into crowded supermarkets, high as all hell. High on life, we make eyes with fly strangers, the hope in our faces burning bright. Up, down, and around the block, winning lost souls in some holy dance. It's bigger than man's stupid reasoning, trumps pop psychology with the flick of a verse. It's the brand of sainthood you've always desired and didn't know it. Am I right? I'm bringing it right now and you love it. I know you do. Talk to me. You want a movement? Well, here it is. It's time to stand for more than your inebriated self. Think about it. Find yourself immersed in something great, the sort of thing that might pull a poem out of you, maybe even a good one, with meter, like iambic or something. This thing we'll fight for, this magnificent monster of a movement complete with mad bumper stickers and quality tracts, anointed handkerchiefs and ink pens; this thing with more grape juice concentrate; this thing that offers what no gang ever could, not ever; this with no name as of yet, more on that later, but a soul and heart that supersedes definition and encompasses belonging. Friendship and camaraderie," Domingo said. "Cookouts and sing-songs. This thing, this bloody beautiful thing we build, could be undeniably, unequivocally, the jam." I laughed my head off, Tomás made the sign of the cross. Domingo bowed and ran for the toilet. This is the kind of foolishness you spew when you're dumb high and a poet.

WHEN I THINK OF MY OLD CREW, I also think of Odd Future. Led by Tyler, the Creator, Odd Future Wolf Gang Kill Them All is a kaleidoscope of talent, wits, and defiant disorder. Since first making a name for themselves as teenagers in 2007, they have remained outliers, a few dozen in-your-face skate rats with little regard for rules, pop tradition, or anything formulaic. They have been protested against and attacked incessantly for their lyrics, which frequently make references to murder, sex, and drug abuse. Tyler, Earl Sweatshirt, and a few others in the collective have come to represent disruption as a calling card. They are young and rich and free, they "skate hard and thrash black hoodies." They won't be tamed or bent against their will. They are skaters through and through. The ways in which they've challenged authority, especially on their early records, and in interviews, is on par with so many of the youth I know who came of age in challenging circumstances. They can be terrifying for those who don't understand them, but affirming for those of us who do.

Odd Future more or less disbanded after members gained notoriety and started to branch out as single entities. But the same criticisms have followed Tyler and Earl, specifically, years into their successful solo careers. Neither has shied away from including violent and gruesome subject matter on their albums. As is often the case with these things, there is far more to unpack than what can possibly be understood at the surface. Both rappers, in fact, have attributed much of their anger and disillusionment to the void left by their absent fathers. The pain of abandonment is something the rappers still carry, however explicitly, as they have settled into adulthood. Much of their material explores these frustrations candidly, their deft and cutting verses serving as portals into the broader epidemic that is fatherlessness in America. But this is what ultimately powered the creative spirit of Odd Future when they started. "It made for good music when we were angsty teens," Earl told the *Los Angeles Times*. "Daddy problems are tight when you're trying to make angsty music."

For them, it was about confronting personal demons while also creating something that resonated on the level of art. It becomes increasingly clear that, had OF members not gravitated to the counterculture early on, there might have been nothing else to help light their paths. In these art forms, they found a kind of refuge, a vehicle for their aggression. But this is the reality of millions of youth everywhere, not just rap stars or skaters raised in fractured homes. Every day boys and girls are left to make it work, to try and build their lives with pieces that don't fit neatly together. This is why fathers on a whole have such positional power. Everything a father does matters. Their words, and their silences, are universes unto themselves.

To let Earl tell it on "Chum":

> It's probably been twelve years since my father left,
>   left me fatherless
> And I just used to say I hate him in dishonest jest

The counterculture took the place of a father I could no longer touch. Since things like school and religion couldn't get through to me, I was being trained up outside of organized institutions. What I gravitated to were these movements that not only felt redeeming, but also freeing. They were almost everything I needed.

4

In Thebe Neruda Kgositsile's sixth year, his father and former South African National Poet Laureate Keorapetse Kgositsile, played magician, pulling a disappearing act that would leave Thebe scrambling for meaning. Although the boy seemed destined to set the world on fire from a young age, that road was laden with uncertainty. Much later, Thebe would undergo a transformation of his own, emerging as Earl Sweatshirt and becoming one of the most compelling voices of the Internet generation.

Shortly after the release of his 2010 debut mixtape, Earl, *Earl Sweatshirt was exiled out of the country on account of bad behavior. Not uncommon. Except that the timing could not have been more frustrating; not just for Earl but for new devoted fans. Odd Future was buzzing, and Earl's departure from it was shrouded in mystery and confusion. It started when Earl's mother, a civil rights attorney, was desperate to see her son set straight. Her tough love included plans for Earl to study at Coral*

Reef Academy, a therapeutic retreat for at-risk boys in Samoa. The move was met with severe opposition by OF supporters the world over. Thus began "Free Earl," an online campaign aimed at bringing the young poet home. Suffice to say, those efforts were fruitless, and Earl would return to Los Angeles only in due time. When a healthy fear—fear of where his destructive path might lead—drew him to make the necessary changes.

"I didn't have a dad coming up," Earl told the Fader *shortly after returning home. "I didn't have someone to be scared of." The necessity of fear and its ability to instruct was a striking admission coming from the then eighteen-year-old.*

I can dig it . . .

ONE DAY IN THE SUMMER of my sixteenth year, I ambled in the house, the stench of herb covering me like an omen. My stepdad Joe was at work, and the other three boys were out doing their business. And there was Ma, packing my things with a solemn look. The sun warmed the open room, sinking its teeth into our backs. Clothes sat arranged in piles: pants, shirts, a hat and jacket for the cold of my uncle's finca. I'd been with Tomás and Domingo, who came up on some smoke and the DMX record. It was 1997, and I was a house on fire. But Ma was about to make her chess move, and I didn't see it coming. A marathon of a lesson disguised as a vacation.

I hadn't been there in years—Colombia, the land of my parents, the place where'd they'd met and stumbled into love. I figured this trip might just define my youth. Maybe I'd even lose my virginity, which was my biggest hope, something I'd been lying about for years. Most of my friends had already embarked on their sexual careers, or been lying about it, for some time. No matter, it was all we talked about. It was the reason we longed for the best gear, the freshest kicks, got out of bed in the morning.

The next day was a mad rush of last-minute details and making sure all was in order for my trip. Joey wasn't too affected. "Have a great summer, brother," he said. But Alejandro and Andres were sad—their big brother was leaving. At the airport, Ma got wild emotional, too. Tears fell when we approached the security checkpoint and "Ma," I said, "it's only a summer." She nodded, her cheeks pink and her sleeves damp with the stuff of leaving. She was holding both my brothers' hands, struggling to hold it together. I didn't let myself catch feelings, though, no way. I said my goodbyes and shoved off in a dash, knew there was much to gain in this going. All I did then was scribble raps into composition pads and get high with degenerates, lost ones like myself who'd much rather steal cars than plan a life. Carpio was the worst, if we're measuring evil. The sort of cold-hearted drifter people kept away from their crib at all cost. You wouldn't believe the thing he showed us once at his place. I'm talking about pictures of his mother and her man getting busy in the master bedroom, a spacious dwelling bordering her son's, with mirrors all over like some museum. It was disturbing how it happened, the way he flashed the images before us, the specifics of which I'll refrain from detailing, with the casualness it takes to hand someone a coffee. We snuck glances and our eyes grew big. We batted the images away, wondered to ourselves what sort of human it took to flash erotic portraits of his mother in front of degenerates.

MY TÍOS WERE THERE to pick me up at the airport in Colombia. They brought empanadas and I ate in the car while they argued. I noticed everything as we sped through the city. The cars, the beautiful people, the political graffiti adorning every wall from the airport to the city center. I wondered about so much on the drive; mostly about all the contradicting hungers I felt, my dreams. I thought about my father, whom I'd planned to see while in Colombia. And I wondered how long it would take for a dope broad to notice my accent, take me in her arms, and solve the lingering problem that was my virginity. My tío had just procured the 1974 Volkswagen Beetle we were in, and I full-on hated my soul for not having mastered the shift. When the car slowed down, I'd blow kisses out the window, no shame, hungry for the flesh of curvy passersby. I wondered what Tomás and Domingo would be up to while I was befriending new girls, drinking aguardiente with my cousins, and running around in the woods free free free.

When we arrived at the house, my tía led me to the room that would be mine for the coming months. I opened my bags and saw nearly everything I owned, packed ever so tightly like they do in the army. I didn't know many people who'd gone to the army, but I gathered this was how they packed, using every inch of space so as to make room for the last things they might ever see. I put some clothes on hangers and laid out my posters on the bed. I opened the window and felt the cool enter my room, the days before me like a mist. After a while, my tío called out for me to come for lunch. There at the table were my tía and my cousins, Ana and Carolina, the latter which was a year younger than me and gorgeous. Carolina said, "It's good to have you here, did you get settled?" "Almost," I said. I told them I thought it was funny how Ma had packed so many of my things for such a short stay. "I thought you were going to be here for a year?" Ana said. Then my tía gave her a look because Ana had spilled the beans. All their faces went cold, like I was the only one there not privy to my own future. "I'm sorry," my tía said. "I'm so sorry. Your mother thought you might not have boarded. It was a hard decision for her but she made it." She said, "Please understand." She said, "You'll come around, I promise." I looked down at my food, then over at my tío. I got up and went swiftly to my room with the open window to think about this revelation. No wonder she sent me with everything, I thought. Sent the screw-up far off to get rehabilitated. I feared I might get swallowed up by everything that was to come. When you plan on being gone for a summer, there's something of an end in mind. But a year is far too long to see the end of anything, even more when you're sixteen and a virgin.

The next morning, I poured some cereal and sat by the pool, watched the dogs fuss and nibble on something dead. I almost envied them as I wondered what this year would be like. "How's it going?" my tío asked, pulling up a chair. "Fine," I said, looking out at the dogs. "I'm sorry you're angry," he said. "It was hard for your ma," he said, and reached into his bag. "She wanted to tell you herself but that went to hell, no? Anyway, I agreed to let you stay here because your tía and I want the same for you, the best." He said, "Take this," handing me a copy of Franz Kafka's *The Metamorphosis*. "This will help to pass the time."

I finally rang home, listened to Ma preach about how it was all for my good, something I'd understand when I had children of my own to look after. I pleaded and she cried, went on about her reasoning. It was the same drivel I'd heard from my tío, mostly, but with pain behind it. Classes would start in just over a month at the technical school downtown. Some summer. *You'll be OK,* everyone told me. But they didn't know anything. I never told them that.

Nights I spent wandering the city with my cousins and their friends, real lookers but all with novios, meaning they had boyfriends. One of them, this dark flaca with long fat curls, gave me an overly friendly eye one night. It could have just been the wind kissing her face as we stood underneath a tree with hamburgers. On one of those nights I met Monkey, who was crazy, and who gave me a nickname: the Gringo. He'd say, *Yo, Gringo, would you like to go dancing to the disco tech?* He planned to perfect his English and someday live near the beach in Miami. I gathered we'd get along well. He liked hip-hop and the Sex Pistols and Rage Against the Machine. We'd go to the club or lounge or pool hall and I'd pass out drunk in a corner. It went like this until I visited my new school for an orientation.

Ana and Carolina attended a prep school adorned with red brick and cobblestone, a specimen of Spanish colonial architecture. The students wore uniforms, and everyone there bothered about cleanliness. The technical school, my school, was different; it was held in a smaller building where you couldn't see the graffiti from the outside. Monkey ran the joint; he had this air about him.

School took some adjusting, grasping formulas in Spanish and all that. Also, I was smoking roll-ups with Monkey and this kid they called Gordo behind the garbage almost every day. Sometimes Alejo would join us, but I could have done without him and his loose tongue. He had it bad for Carolina and often went too far about that in my presence. I almost socked him hard once, but Monkey calmed me down and urged Alejo to refrain from mentioning Carolina in the Gringo's presence. Monkey functioned as the head of our crew. He was seventeen and bald by choice, unpredictable as death itself. Everything he did seemed exaggerated. His tone of voice; his partiality to weekends; his excitement at someone's acquisition of a sort of smoke he'd never tried. And though he was basically likable, he made some people uneasy.

Monkey invited us to his house in Dosquebradas. This was a part of town I'd heard about before from Ma and my tía. They said it was no good. *It's filthy,* they told me. *Don't ever go there.* I met up with Gordo, who lived just up the hill, near the tennis courts. He paid our bus fare and shot me a wink, said to get the next one and we were square. On the ride, I thought to inquire about Dosquebradas, about the neighborhood. To avoid seeming overly concerned about my safety, I said nothing. The bus left us on a run-down back road across from an abandoned learning center. The whole thing reminded me of the scene in *Boyz n the Hood* where the boys case the dead body tucked away in the bushes. There was no dead body here as far as I knew, and anyway, we were a long way from South Central Los Angeles. This was Dosquebradas.

Walking down the dirt path, just Gordo and me, down to El Poblado in the light rain, we went to see Monkey.

My thing was this: I wanted to please home but also to bend rules, break things, build and destroy. I wanted to smoke and have females; I wanted to piss off people I despised. But also I wanted to rhyme and write stories, make bookoo bucks and make Ma and Joe proud. My father, damn, I could care less. At least that's what I told myself.

When we got there, Monkey was on the steps smoking a cigarette; no shirt on, plastic bags wrapped over his shoes. He was obsessive when it came to footwear, and he did everything to protect his Nikes from smudge or rain. I could relate. We talked some and then went inside to look at television. Monkey told us he'd just seen on the news that the guerrillas had kidnapped and executed an American Bible translator named Chester something or other who they believed was working with the CIA. They looked at me like I was supposed to know something. Monkey went to change and Gordo for the kitchen. I remember thinking it was odd, this Gordo just rummaging through the refrigerator. I watched as he examined its contents with the intensity it must take to perform an autopsy. He made himself a ham sandwich and sat on the couch opposite me. I opened my knapsack and thumbed through the book my tío had given me the day I arrived. Finally, Monkey came out and said, "Ah, Gringo, as Gregor Samsa awoke one morning from uneasy dreams he found himself transformed in his bed into a gigantic insect." My eyes froze. Monkey pointed to his bookshelf and there sat half a dozen copies of *The Metamorphosis* in various languages.

We got blasted at Monkey's and went out, our eyes peeled for the best girls. The streets were crowded, all of us just drinking and yelling at cars as they passed. Music thundered from houses, mostly American rock music. Gordo asked me did I know Pink Floyd personally and I said no, and laughed to myself. Really the area wasn't all that bad like I'd heard. A few fights almost broke out by the pool hall, but it was nothing I wasn't used to. It felt familiar. Just a bunch of street-talking teenagers killing time in the Colombian night, which to them was just the night.

In the morning, Carolina burst into my room and asked if I'd been in Dosquebradas with Monkey. "Who told you that?" "My friend told me she saw you and Monkey with a fat kid and that you were blitzed walking around El Poblado." "So what?" "Well, you better not bring that trash into this house," she said, "or Papi will send you packing." She left and I watched the ceiling fan spin for the better part of an hour.

Most days it was just me, Monkey, and Gordo. We smoked at Monkey's, watched David Lynch films at Monkey's, ate and got into philosophical exchanges at Monkey's. The more I got to know him, the more I realized why people thought him a pestilence. His behavior was intense, even infectious. There was something that got into those he befriended, like a spell that drove you to his side, drove you to listen to his stories and kill entire afternoons on his couch. He was smart, too, and he reminded me some of Tomás. Still, there was so much to question. For one, you wondered where Monkey's mother was all the time. For all the days I spent at her house I never saw her once. He said she worked a lot. But I was there all kinds of hours for many months, and it seemed impossible for anyone to work that much. I only saw her in pictures; pictures of her and little Monkey, pictures of her and Monkey's father, who I was told died long ago over some misunderstanding involving drugs. So much in Monkey's world was a fog. And when you asked him something about anything, he had a way of confusing you more.

On a Saturday afternoon, Monkey asked me if I wanted to live at his house; he said that I could move in if I wanted to. We were out front, looking at old magazines. He made a comment about *Eraserhead* that I can't remember. Monkey was more fidgety than normal and he looked like he hadn't washed in days. I got the sense he was lonely, like he had no one in his life with whom he could be frank, like a brother. He didn't look up when he asked about the moving in, as if he were ashamed; ashamed because he needed someone around to keep him in check so he wouldn't do anything rash; like the time he beat a boy senseless and pissed on him, or the time he set a neighbor's cat on fire for kicks. I told him that I couldn't because my tíos were paying for me to study, and because of that, I felt I had a duty to remain under their roof. That's the reason I gave, a sensible one I thought. I almost offered to let him stay at my pad, but then I remembered I didn't have one. I didn't have anything.

On the loneliest days—and there were many of them—I'd lock myself in my room, crack open the window, and fall back, letting beats play out of a small radio. The music fed me, conquered me, led, misled, pushed, prodded, angered, comforted, and convicted. And while I often felt dejected, the truth is my friends spanned all across the map.

They were: Nas, Public Enemy, A Tribe Called Quest, De La Soul, Wu-Tang Clan, Cypress Hill, Poor Righteous Teachers, Group Home, the Roots, Busta Rhymes, Goodie Mob, Outkast, Common Sense, Mobb Deep, Smif-N-Wessun, AZ, Fat Joe, Erick Sermon, Redman, Keith Murray, the Notorious B.I.G., Gang Starr, Digable Planets, Tupac, Organized Konfusion, the Fugees, Brand Nubian,

Bahamadia, Boogiemonsters, Da Bush Babees, O.C., Company Flow, Jurassic Five, Jay-Z, Cru, Slum Village.

Lyrics constantly swirled around in my head, no matter what I was doing. I could be walking around El Poblado, or in the shower, or hopelessly stuck in a conversation. I was an escapist, longing only to be found in the ruminations of my heroes. Everything called back to the music. If I overheard someone on the television say, "First things first," I automatically thought, *I Poppa—freaks all the honies.* If a classmate said, "Pass it over here," I would respond with "Tical," quoting Method Man to def ears. If nothing else, I had that. Growing up, I would always hear stories of unhappy kids who ran away from home for one reason or another. But I preferred to close my eyes and turn the volume up to the max. It kept me sane.

THE MEMORY ENDURES of the single night I tried to run away from home and failed. It was usually my white friends who did mess like that and I mostly couldn't relate. No matter how bad it got, Ma's food, for one, was too good for me to even consider leaving for real. And I never thought slipping out the back door like some fake ninja would solve much. But this night, the idea wouldn't leave my bone head.

First, some backstory:

A few days before that attempt to run away, I'd gotten arrested for breaking and entering. The word at school was that there was an abandoned house near the Boys Club where we could smoke and play cards. After last period, I met up with a classmate near the spot. But I didn't know other people were coming too, certainly not goons like these. Judging by how easily the MacGyver of the bunch unlocked the deadbolt, it was obvious he'd done this before. We all strolled right in and marveled at the freedom of an empty house. Someone had a radio in their bag and turned on Power 96. Clouds of smoke filled the room, and we played tunk and dominoes. For a short while, it was perfect. But our fun was interrupted when, less than an hour later, we heard police sirens outside. Cops started yelling and pounding on the door; everyone panicked. A girl yelled, "I can't go back to jail!" Her boyfriend told her to shut the hell up and we all bolted out the side like imbeciles. We didn't get far; half a dozen cops, who were all faster and twice as big, closed in on us. One caught me in the jaw and threw me to the ground. He kicked my tail hard as a kick drum from Pete Rock. Charges were filed and I was put on house arrest. I never found out what happened to the others, and I wouldn't see most of them ever again. I just knew that outside of attending school, I wasn't permitted to leave the house for three months. Strangely, they didn't give me one of those ankle monitors I'd seen other people wear.

So on this night, I packed a few things in a JanSport and left home just after eleven o'clock. My plan was to crash at Carpio's place for a few days until I figured out my next move. His mom wouldn't even notice, I thought, given that she didn't pay much mind to her own son. His house was several miles away and I knew I couldn't walk the whole way. After a while I came upon a bicycle that would take me the remainder of the distance. I snatched bikes back then like Kenny Lofton stole bases.

By the time I reached Carpio's, it was nearly midnight. I started throwing small rocks at his window hoping to wake him up. Rock after rock, and nothing. I must have thrown close to fifty before his mom opened the door, in her bra and panties.

"Diablo, muchacho!" she said. "¿Qué estás haciendo?"

"Uh, sorry. Is Carpio home?"

"You didn't know, mijo? Ese idiota está en la cárcel." That idiot is in jail.

She slammed the door and I hopped back on the Huffy. I had nowhere to go, so I headed back home, the city dark and tranquil. I slept for two hours before it was time to get up and get ready for school. Nobody had even noticed I was gone.

A few weeks later, Carpio got out. "I heard you came to see me," he said.

"Me?"

"My mom said you were throwing rocks at the window in the middle of the night."

"Your mom is tripping, that definitely wasn't me."

DAYS PASSED and I didn't hear from Monkey. I asked Gordo if he had, and he said no. I even asked the worthless Alejo, who said, "I don't know about that, Gringo, nor do I give a care, but I'm going to see about a job." And then, as if on cue, he asked about my cousin Carolina and I walked away. That night I thought about what Monkey had asked me, about the expression on his face and how lonely he'd seemed, about all the things I'd felt since arriving in Colombia; my different hungers and rap fantasies, and also about how maybe being a virgin wasn't the worst thing—that I could be as lonely as Monkey, who was definitely not a virgin, and still be miserable.

Weeks glided by and still no Monkey. I took the bus to his house only to discover he wasn't there. I wandered around El Poblado with my bag of Kafka and went into one of the cafés. I asked the woman at the register if she knew who Monkey was, and she said she'd never in her life heard of such a thing as a boy called Monkey. When I exited the café, I saw him. I saw Monkey in front of a fruit stand nursing a joint. He was holding a book, and halfway listening to a homeless man who was mumbling something unintelligible. Monkey's clothes were filthy, and he seemed even more anxious than he had the night he asked if I wanted to move into his house. When I asked him where he'd been, he barely looked at me, as if I were a stranger, like I hadn't been with him nearly every day for months. He said he'd been visiting with some family across town. He drew from his smoke and glanced up at me. And that was when he told me he'd found God.

The following day or maybe two days later, Monkey and Gordo were parleying in front of the school. Monkey bright and animated, collected as ever. His clothes were like new and his head cleanly shaven. A few nights prior he looked like he'd been to the pit. Here he was now, swagged out and quoting the Pharcyde. "There she goes again, the dopest Ethiopian," he said to a girl who strolled past. Then the bell sounded and we went into Math with no mention of Monkey's disappearance, or his newfound divine awareness. And that was that. Things returned mostly to their normal order: eating at Monkey's, arguing the state of the world at Monkey's.

I told Gordo what Monkey had said to me, and Gordo said, "Listen." He said that Monkey had found God several times; under his bed, on the bus, in the back of the same dirty pool hall. Gordo said, "Gringo, don't worry about Monkey. This is the way he is. He operates on a spiritual level; a level you will never understand." I dropped it, determined not to worry myself over something that didn't concern me.

MUCH LATER, a few hundred cigarettes later, dozens of visits to Monkey's later, annoying interrogations by my inquisitive cousin later, weeks upon weeks of skipping out on classes later, my tío brought me a letter that had arrived in the mail. It was made out to me but must have been dropped in the mailbox. No name, no return address. I opened it and straightaway knew it was from Monkey. His handwriting was distinct, which is to say it was awful. It was a long letter full of secrets and confessions he'd supposedly never told anyone. He told me he was leaving, that he'd be back someday, but that he'd spoken to God and that he was leaving, running off with Clara, the girl he'd gotten pregnant. He said that if it was a boy he was going to name him Juan. He went on about what a dear friend I'd been and he thanked me for the CDs I'd given him, the Roots and Jeru the Damaja. He told me that his mother had died many years ago, that he was raised by his grandparents and that they'd left him the house and some money before they died. When I finished reading the letter, I placed it in a shoebox and stretched out on the floor. I couldn't believe what I'd read. I couldn't believe he was leaving. Monkey who lived in Dosquebradas, in the neighborhood called El Poblado, Monkey who was a maniac, the only bald seventeen-year-old I'd ever known. The same Monkey who'd asked me to live at his house so that, as I now understood, I could be there for him. My tío walked in and asked if I was OK. I said I was but that a schoolmate was moving away, and that I was sad. He told me I'd have plenty more friends, that this was the cycle of life, people walking in and out, some leaving more of an impression than others. We went into the dining room, where my tía and my cousins, Ana and Carolina, were waiting. They said there had been a phone call, and that my father unfortunately wasn't coming up. I ate well and something like emptiness washed over me.

It was my last weekend in Colombia and, somehow, I was still a virgin. To my mind, it was simply inexcusable. I'd had the opportunity to make a move on a few occasions but something always interrupted the moment. Then, as if the heavenly hosts looked down upon my great lust and had pity, this fine girl pushed through the door. She introduced herself as Camila and said she'd been hired to clean the house that afternoon. Camila was about my age, with soft, caramel skin that made me think of silk. "Go ahead," I told her, sheepishly. Was this my opportunity? Every teenage fantasy came rushing into my mind. I tried to assess the situation and determine the best course of action.

I was watching television in the bedroom when she began to sweep the hall just outside the door. I wanted nothing more than to walk over with something that resembled confidence, take her on the sofa like I was someone else. I thought about it for close to an hour, considering the possible outcomes. There were only two, really. Either Camila would invite the boy from America to enter her while at her workplace or she'd deny him, push him away and share the account with her employers, in which the boy, the reckless nephew, would be shamed beyond measure. By the time the daydream ended, she'd excused herself and left out the door. For the next hour, I listened to the Pink Floyd song "Young Lust" and smoked Marlboros on the ground.

"I am just a new boy / Stranger in this town / Where are all the good times? / Who's gonna show this stranger around?"

SEEING CAMILA DO HER THING reminded me of Ma's side hustle days. Some weekends she would leave my brothers with a friend and take me with her to tidy up rich people's homes. Again, Ma did what she could to supplement income whenever the opportunity came. Whether it was hemming dresses or mopping floors, it was all the same. Usually Ma's well-off salon customers were the ones who wanted help, and because they knew Ma's situation, they figured paying for cleaning services was a way to lend a hand. She'd clean two or three houses back to back, about twice a month. I would sit around watching television on big screens, eating candy, and drinking Pepsi. Ma was meticulous, always making sure she went above and beyond what was asked. She had a grace about her that I always thought beautiful. It didn't matter if she was cleaning for a stranger or cooking meals for her sons.

One time, Ma had to do a night job because the owners were returning from vacation early and it was the one house she hadn't yet cleaned. I had to tag along, of course. Problem was, it was June 13, 1989, which meant Game 4 of the NBA Finals between the Detroit Pistons and the Los Angeles Lakers. The Pistons were up 3–0, so this was likely to be the end of the road for the Lakers.

And that would mean Kareem Abdul-Jabbar's final game, as he'd announced his retirement at the beginning of the season. I was a Knicks fan then, but I always went ape watching Magic be Magic, and Isaiah Thomas was my second-favorite basketball player behind Michael Jordan. I'd been looking forward to the matchup all day. I brought my Nerf hoop to this Coral Gables mansion and attached it to the front door so I could watch and reenact buckets. I got a kick out of emulating the players' moves, practicing hook shots and fadeaways while Ma went to work with the Fabuloso. I remember James Worthy was lighting it up, taking John Salley to the hole and sinking jumpers nonstop. In the third quarter, Worthy blocked a shot attempt by Mark Aguirre, slamming the ball against the backboard. I got carried away reenacting the play and knocked over an expensive dish that was displayed on a mantel next to the television. When Ma heard the crash, she came running in. I just stood there, mouth agape. I don't recall if Ma beat me afterward, but I do remember she refused to accept payment for her two hours of work because of my clumsy move. The Lakers ended up getting swept, and I watched Kareem walk off the hardwood for the last time.

Anyhow. Colombia. My tío's house. Still a virgin. Summer ending.

When my tío came in from work, he flipped the record to "Is There Anybody Out There?" He said he preferred the melancholy of Roger Waters on lead. The instrumental part of the song, he said, reminded him of sex with his wife when they were teenagers. He told me to ask her later what Pink Floyd reminded her of and I laughed and said I would do no such thing. I thumbed through a biography of Woody Allen and we ate sandwiches on the balcony. Later, my tío asked what I wanted to do. I said that we could stay in or go out, that it didn't matter to me. He said, "No, I mean with your life." He said, "What do you want?" I didn't know how to answer. There were so many things I wanted but, in that moment, I couldn't recall any of them.

5

WHEN I TOUCHED BACK DOWN IN BROWARD, it felt as though I'd been given new vision. Almost a year had passed, and Domingo was mostly doing the same ratchet mess. Tomás on the other hand, always the more pragmatic of us, had elevated. He'd secured a position at a bank and was moving up the ranks. We were still squad, naturally, and kicked it on the weekends. But in time the three of us began to devote more attention to our individual pursuits. Tomás's gift for business made it so that, before long, he was helping his mother with expenses. Months dragged on and I kept filling composition books with rhymes, plugging away in class and on the bus. Stories, too; I would day after day string words together, shout my truth at the dead air until the fervency in my tone made me feel powerful. In those moments, I was more than a boy at war, more than a son abandoned. I was a planet unto myself, suspended but moving steadily toward the sun. There were flames on my pen, and flames on my tongue. I knew the present and future were in my clutches. If I could only cling to that when mischief called.

Domingo dropped out junior year and told us he was enlisting in the army. His parents had split while I was gone; his father had a lot in common with my own. But his mother was ecstatic about her son's decision, Domingo said. We saw the pride he felt at the thought of making his mother proud. "Your Dominican ass ain't gonna last through Basic Training," Tomás offered, and we cracked up. We hit Riverside with two Dutch Masters and listened to instrumentals; we talked about how much we missed these nights, these carefree nights before the so-called future was biting at our heels.

The seeds of real change were planted when Ma, weeks later, had an acquaintance of hers, a *believer* as she described her, lay hands on me. You need God, Ma had told me, a phrase I'd never heard her use before. Without my consent, she arranged for the woman, this *prayer warrior,* to drop by on a Saturday to beat the sin out of me. "You shed most of it back in Colombia, gracias a Dios," Ma said pointedly, "but some is still lingering." She was right.

When the woman arrived that morning, she introduced herself and placed a chair in the center of my room. "Sit down," she said in a kind voice, producing a bottle of anointing oil from her Champion hoodie. Dread came over me, an apprehension unlike any I'd ever felt. What was this? And why now? Then, as if summoning the power of heaven and hell both in her tiny hands and mouth, the woman erupted in an invocation that thundered like slam poetry. I felt the weight of her words press upon my entire body and could move not a single muscle. Worse still, her words were dead-on in respect to where I was mentally and emotionally. She saw directly inside of me, this little woman—my lust, my dreams, the hatred I felt for my father, all fathers—and spoke it all back to me in new and bone-chilling language. When she was through, although in truth I sometimes imagine she's still going, the woman retrieved a small Old Testament from her bag and set it firmly on the desk. She opened it to Psalms 91 and excused herself. As foreign as the whole episode was to me, I couldn't help but feel as though some indistinct force were drawing me to itself.

IN THE WEEKS THAT FOLLOWED I began to study the Scriptures with a curious enthusiasm. In Pereira, I'd begun to fall in love with literature, thanks in large part to those solitary afternoons reading Gabriel García Márquez and Kafka—"Literature begins and ends with *The Metamorphosis*," my uncle had said. But the Bible was thoroughly different. This was saints, sinners, and the blood of the lamb shed to cover the multitude of our transgressions. I was taken aback by the supposed Good Book's large and ardent claims. I started to connect the theological references in some of the music I loved best, from Poor Righteous Teachers to the Fugees. Something was happening in me, but I didn't know what it was. I thought about Monkey and his God business; I considered old Sunday school lessons I'd long deemed meaningless; I wondered about my boys and what they might say. What would I tell them? Before I could make up my mind, before I could tell them this trash-talking Henny sipper was suddenly on some faith trip, a few cats I occasionally played ball with invited me to a youth revival out of the clear blue sky. "Come out and check the service," said Jacob, who was half-Mexican but looked Filipino. "Wednesday night," he said. "I'll pick you up. We shoot hoops and rhyme after." Those were my greatest obsessions, so I accepted the invitation, half-understanding that I'd just agreed to attend church.

Ma's friend, the random invite from Jacob. Again it felt like I was being pursued by something. And thus began the campaign for ownership of my soul and mind.

Jacob and Konata pulled up to the house in a midnight-blue Maxima. "Nice ride," I said as I climbed into the back seat. Jacob was a couple of years older than me and had recently graduated from Piper, a rival school. Konata hailed from Brooklyn but had moved to Broward some years prior, with his mother and sister. He was auditing classes at the community college and worked part-time at an Army Navy store. Both were part of a loose group I'd seen at the basketball court on and off since junior high. We'd run back-to-back games and talk rap and movies, but that was the extent of our friendship at the time.

Tunes were pumping in Jacob's car, but it wasn't anything I recognized. I inquired about the voice busting on the tape. "That's K-Nuff," Jacob said, looking to Konata. "He's in a group called Nuff Wisdom." I turned to Konata, excitedly. "Word?" "That's me," he answered matter-of-factly. "The next verse is Danny," he said. "We call him Wisdom for some reason." They laughed and Konata cranked the volume. I let down my window and gave ear. The raps centered mostly on God and girls. There was mention of a father who'd bounced without warning. It all sounded achingly familiar.

WHEN WE APPROACHED THE BUILDING, I felt my insides start to turn. I wanted a Newport something serious. I'd been low on cash and wasn't able to pick up smokes that morning. As we made our way into the youth wing, which felt as brisk as a hospital waiting room, I was struck by the sight of more than two hundred teenagers singing, their arms outstretched in unison. Days before, I'd been lifted on hash in a stolen Oldsmobile Cutlass with a pack of heathens, and here I was now in the thick of a revival.

I want to say that, in the seventeen years leading up to this meeting, I had seen the devil. I had seen the devil many times. I had seen him in my self-centeredness; I had seen him in the faces of the homicidal men who wanted to hurt my family; I had seen him in my father's bloodshot eyes when he was twisted and far gone; I had seen him in the older boy who'd put that blade to my neck after I mouthed off at him. I had not, conversely, ever seen anything I'd considered to be God. I had not seen what to my view was His mighty hand at work; I had not seen the lame get up and walk; I had not even seen, for that matter, His followers amount to any city on a hill, which I'd read about in the New Testament. No, up until then, I had seen only abandoned children, pistol whippings outside the bodega, and mothers doing their absolute best in a world in want of good men. But on this night, my eyes beheld something that I perceived as beautiful. These were youths marked not by their miseducation but by something else. I stood myself in awe as they sought the blessing of heaven in song and in their exchanges with one another. Even the way they engaged the sermon, delivered by a young preacher called Jon, who also happened to rhyme and was known to some as Kid Invision, made an impression. "It's all God," they told me later when I said how gifted a speaker I thought Jon was. "It's all God," I repeated, pretending to understand.

MY CONCEPTION OF RELIGION was distant and almost amusingly uninformed. Over the years I'd imagined angels and hell's demons occupied in a perpetual spiritual joust. And a judge who didn't bother much to insert Himself into petty human dealings. But I also wasn't particularly concerned, as none of it seemed to offer any meaning to my day-to-day reality. With no clear rationalization, I'd subscribed to a gospel of indifference, which, by my account, was crippling in itself. But after the service, the possibility that there might be more to unearth began to take root in me.

An inexplicable emotional peace invaded my mind as the days ensued. The holy ghost became something I could hope to access. Which is not to say that I no longer held bitterness in my heart, but that peace and deep rage could work interchangeably in my soul. If I felt the need to let anger flow from me in order to survive, it would be there, I reasoned. If I resolved to turn the other cheek on an enemy, it would be so. But it could not have been possible without my hearing the message about living as peacemakers in a war-torn world. While I didn't yet grasp the nuance packed in every scriptural quotation, I can say with certainty that what brought me back the next week was the words.

For me, it was always about words. The biblical anecdotes and wrenching one-liners tugged at something in me. Like the hip-hop I so prized, there was a poetic richness to the stories and to the exhortations that seeped into me. After my third visit to the youth group, while overcome with emotion at Jon's talk, I told the god of the sun, moon, and stars that I'd give up weed forever. My intentions were pure, but I felt the war well up inside me as I left the building and went back out into the world. I felt the war in me like I'd always had.

From then on, I was tested almost daily. All at once there was good herb brought back from California—"Hit this," a classmate said. There was a perfect girl that wanted to get busy; there were after-school brawls I could not avoid. There was real life beyond the walls of some sanctuary, as there always had been.

ON A WARM AND HUMID NIGHT, I had a craving for Entenmann's chocolate chip cookies and decided to make the short trip to the grocery store. With a few bucks on me, I thought it a fair idea to treat myself. Off I went, Mobb Deep ringing in my headphones the whole way. Havoc and Prodigy's street tales were a fitting backdrop for a night trek. At the store, I bought the box of cookies and a pack of smokes. As I made my way through the emptying parking lot en route back to the house, I spotted a shopping cart in the distance. There was something in it, I saw, something I figured had been left behind mistakenly, and curiosity led me to it. It was a black leather purse, unzipped, with a Gucci pocketbook exposed.

I opened it and saw a stack of crisp hundred-dollar bills poking out. I counted them slowly, one by one. There were nine in total. There were also credit cards, receipts, a shopping list. But, and much to my annoyance, there was a driver's license. Which meant that the purse belonged to someone with a face and an identity and contact information who could be located if the finder had any compassion in them whatever. I wrestled for close to a minute, holding the cookies and cigarettes that represented the last of my fortune. What would I do? Had this happened just months before, had I come upon this not-so-buried treasure as my normal self, I'd have charged the credit cards and spent the money with abandon. I could see the mall from where I stood. But I had become new, I told myself. I was different now. I went inside to find the manager to tell him what I'd found. The woman was called and she arrived minutes later to claim her belongings. I stood around, anticipating a major reward. When the manager pointed me out, the woman thanked me and handed me a ten-dollar bill. She sped off in a black Cadillac Escalade and I walked home in the night.

When I arrived—anxious to tell everyone about my virtuous deed as further proof that I had changed—I learned that my tío Carlos, engulfed by the Sadness, had tried to commit suicide. All they said was that his wife found him in the bathtub, and he was narrowly saved by a team of paramedics. He was bipolar II, I learned, like Ma's father. The following week, we learned that my primo Juan Carlos had put a gun to his head. He'd been under a lot of pressure at his law firm and the stress got to him. The Sadness, I came to understand, had had its way with my family for generations.

THE DAY MY COUSIN TOOK HIS OWN LIFE, I shut out the world. My chest was hot with anger and despair. I roamed about school like a loner, like a monk devoted exclusively to his interior life. I didn't play the wall—it was always the chicos and black kids on one wall and the jocks and preppies on another—and kept to my music. I passed on the lunch break cypher of which I was always a part. I didn't circle the breakers who congregated outside the gym after fourth period. It was me and my Discman. I had the new *Mos Def & Talib Kweli Are Black Star* album, my therapy as I wandered the halls and football field instead of dozing in Geometry. "Respiration" got me in my feelings—it was timely. Kweli: "Hard to be a spiritual being when shit is shaking what you believe in." With that, I felt justified in my confusion. I wanted to embrace spirituality but everything around me was off. I found it difficult to reconcile faith with my own deep-seated issues, and with the meaninglessness of suffering in my world. I thought I'd gotten over certain things that had troubled me for years, things that I'd suppressed for fear of having to confront them. I sat on the bleachers and wept. I wept for myself, for my uncle, my cousin, for Monkey, and for Domingo; I wept for my brothers and for Ma, who, although she was happy with Joe, had a quiet sadness about her. Joy and contentment seemed beyond grasp. I couldn't understand why my uncle wanted to die, and why Juan Carlos didn't get help. I couldn't understand why my father didn't want me. And I despised him for not being around to show me what pain means.

Joe never disciplined any of us by his hand. He spoke sternly when necessary, but he wouldn't succumb to violence, not even on his own son. But beatings were normal for me and my brothers when we were smaller. For those of us who grew up under the reign of La Chancla, the concept of corporal punishment was not alien. From the moment we could speak in full sentences, we knew the sting of hard discipline. When we got out of line—be it at the market, the post office, anywhere—a good whooping was to be expected. Shoes, rulers, spatulas—these were the objects with which many of us, the children of immigrants, were instructed to stop pestering our siblings and/or improve our grades. Throughout our adolescence, my brothers and I grew acquainted with the purple belt our mother took to our bodies to curb bad behavior. She kept it in a high place in her closet, and for a time, we feared it. It wasn't that our mothers were attempting to inflict serious or lasting pain. No, it was more a question of traditions, about applying the same methods of child-rearing their parents had applied to them. So on and so forth. But Joe wasn't raised this way, and only once did he put his hands on me in anger.

ONE SATURDAY, I was out well past curfew and didn't bother to call. When I returned home, Joe was sitting at the dining room table, waiting. He was nursing a glass of scotch, like he typically did before retiring each night. He'd sent Ma upstairs to bed sometime earlier, told her she'd worried over me enough for two lifetimes. "I'll take care it," he insisted.

It was 1 a.m. when the jangle of my keys woke Joe.

"Where were you?" he called out from the black as I shut the door behind me.

"What?"

"Where the hell were you?" he repeated, sizing me up.

"Anyway," I said dismissively.

I tried to make my way up the stairs toward my room, but he grabbed my shoulder and stopped me in my tracks.

"Take your hands off me, I'm serious."

"Or else what?" he threatened.

I USED TO LIVE FOR CONFRONTATION, if you want to know the truth. I'd built a reputation among friends for never flaking out when things popped off, even if it wasn't in my best interest to take it there. I won some fights, and I lost many others. With Joe, I had no interest in entertaining any drama or creating more awkwardness between us. As I'd gotten older, we simply landed on a comfortable rhythm of staying out of each other's path. We maneuvered on separate playing fields, and were bound to schedules that did not coincide. I respected this man who took me on trips as a boy and had treated me like a son; who'd always looked past my brazenness and made me feel significant; who could take a divorced woman with three children and love them as his own, and who never made them feel lesser for any reason. But still, I had my life, and I didn't feel the need to explain myself.

Joe has a medium build, and stands just under six feet. Back then, he could subdue me without any great effort, which I didn't realize until it came time for him to show it. When I went to push him away, he caught my wrist and shoved me against the refrigerator. He looked into my eyes and demanded that I respect his house. That I never again undermine his and my mother's rules while under their roof. My hands shook at my side, not with fear but with reverence. In his face, I saw a man who'd had enough of my unruliness, a man who in his fifty-plus years had experienced his own torment, from a chaotic childhood in Uniontown, Pennsylvania, to witnessing unimaginable horrors in the Vietnam War; who became a widower in his mid-thirties; who'd toiled all his life and was not going to let anyone make him feel inferior in his own home. A surge of adrenaline rose from my stomach enabling me to break loose. I charged out the door. It was nearly two in the morning now. I walked around the block brooding the dumpster fire that was my life until I'd cooled off. When I returned, all was quiet and still.

I WAS HANGING with the church crew more and more. Domingo left for Basic Training and Tomás had taken a second job as a school crossing guard. Carpio got locked up for drug possession and armed robbery and was sentenced to three to five years. My somewhat feverish conversion created some distance between me and Tomás. Some days it didn't bother me, but other days it did. Though I mostly stayed broke, I'd managed to fill up five notebooks of short stories, poems, and lyrics to dozens of original songs. But they were just words on pages. At night, I fantasized about the possibility of making actual recordings.

I was invited to a studio session by Nuff Wisdom. Their producer,

Luis—whom they dubbed Chewy—was making beats one day on a borrowed drum machine and they asked me to contribute some bars. We met at Chewy's home studio, the spare room of his two-bedroom flat in Margate. We shot the breeze, had a brainstorm, and retreated to our corners to cook up our parts. The chemistry between the four of us was instantaneous, and by night's end we had three tracks laid down. Although I'd written ample material throughout the years, I'd never recorded on proper equipment. I tried to mask my beginner's zeal, but there was no way around it: I was soaring. Over the telephone the next day it was decided that we would form a group. In my old crew, I was the only one serious about rhyming, so this was new. Now I had comrades I could grow with. I studied MCs and the free-flowing writings of the Beat Generation, intentional in my attempts to get better and make a name. I learned that good songs, not unlike the best poems, have an architecture about them. They are rooms with open spaces and well-lit corridors that lead to higher levels of meaning and consciousness.

Soon our first obstacle presented itself: Chewy had to return the SP-1200 to its owner. With only a mic, a modest keyboard, and nothing with which to create our beats, we were at a standstill. Something had to be done. The four of us drove to Sam Ash with no set plan. We drifted up and down the aisles, coveting the expensive machinery—turntables, subwoofers, elaborate mixing consoles that cost what it might to feed a small country. In a moment of extraordinary foolishness, Chewy, the only one of us with plastic, offered to charge an Akai MPC2000 drum machine to his credit card if we agreed to chip in $50 a month each to pay for it. I'd stopped dealing a long time ago and had no stream of income.

But I did what any eager artist in my position would have done: I committed to paying my portion with no clue as to how I'd swing it. Within minutes we were beaming out of the store, ready to snatch our piece of the world.

ONE OF THE DEACONS from the church had organized what he called a mission trip to New York City and invited us to come along. He'd heard our recording, aptly titled "The Father Song," and thought we'd be an appropriate ice breaker for the week's outreach events. We accepted, told people we were going on tour. That's the word we used: tour. We spent the afternoons going door to door, trudging the Crown Heights neighborhood of Brooklyn handing out flyers. Each night there was a rally, and we were tasked with performing a short set before the main speaker, a Haitian man called Mr. Williams, took the stage. We didn't know how to command a crowd—we were amateurish at best—but it felt good to give it our all. The people were mostly fifty years old and up, but that didn't matter. We felt like we were taking incremental but necessary steps toward something special.

On the final night of the tour, Konata invited his father, who lived nearby, to stop through. He hadn't spoken to his dad in years, but Konata couldn't let the opportunity pass without making contact. Yes, of course he'd be there, his father said. "See you then, my son." Konata was nervous and elated at the same time, and we wondered how long it would take him to spot his father in the crowd.

In the middle of our set, Konata noticed a man enter and take a seat in one of the back pews. "That's him," he whispered to me and

Danny. The man was tall and very thin, with fat dreadlocks that fell straight down his back. He was Rastafarian when Konata was a kid. I looked out at the man and, for an instant, saw my own father. I saw the fathers of all my friends, who'd left behind scars and ruin. I'd never met this man before, but a distaste for him was birthed in me then and there. I hated him for what he had done and for what he had failed to do.

Halfway through "The Father Song"—the hook of which was "Thank you, Father, for bringing me into this earth / but why does it seem you didn't care about my birth?"—Konata and his pops locked eyes. Konata abruptly stopped performing and leapt off the stage, leaving me and Danny and the hundreds in attendance perplexed. Konata walked over to the man, their faces glossy with tears, and the two embraced. The room burst into applause, Pentecostal praise, and fervent prayers for the reunited. People went on about the beauty of forgiveness, about letting go of people's past infractions. My heart, though, was stone-cold. I wasn't ready to forgive a single thing. I felt jealousy and anger, mixed with joy for my friend. The ordeal left me dismayed and I wouldn't shake it for days. But I knew I couldn't live in a state of resentment forever.

That night, I witnessed the binding power of music. I learned that hip-hop, specifically, can be a kind of shape-shifting thing. Not only does it have the agency to unite strangers and move them toward empathy, but it can also draw sons into the arms of their estranged fathers. I saw it happen for Konata. I had to believe it could somehow be the same for me.

Gradually, I saw a world spring to life before me. My perceptivity wide-open, I determined to exert everything into a passion that yielded results. I was prepared to make up for squandered time. The shows got better, and our name began to spread locally, all across South Florida. I was hype.

Graduation loomed and I barely made the minimum grade point average to put high school behind me forever. I took a nothing gig at a skate park, then a clothing store. For many weeks all I did was work, write, and record with a sense of gusto. Time slid without me noticing it and, against my better judgment, I enrolled in college, thinking it might somehow make me a credit to my family. It started off well enough, but during my first semester—I had committed to studying journalism—I got a phone call. A nonprofit missionary organization was sending teams to Central America and they wanted the group to join them, all expenses paid. Chewy had recently gotten married and was unable to steal away. The rest of us renewed our passports, put whatever we were doing on hold, and left for Honduras. For twelve days, we immersed ourselves in the unfamiliar. We saw extreme poverty and incomprehensible wealth; we rocked open air concerts attended by tens of thousands. I filled pages with bad poems about girls, the slang of the ramshackle villages we visited, the smell of the food. One evening I spent hours talking with a homeless man who lived near the square. Later that night when I couldn't sleep, I went out into the hall of the old hotel, which was guarded by policemen armed with assault rifles, and penned my version of the man's sad story as it was told to me.

On the streets they say El Negro Buenavista. *At home, Daddy, what do you have there? These are coins, children, I tell them. These are what we trade for food, I say, and jiggle them so they can hear. They smile and thank me. Then I leave to the corner and come back with a potato or bread. They take a bite and pass it. If they get filled and some is left, I eat. It's nothing. There he is, the people say. The man with the sickly eyes and tattered hair. We pass him each morning en route to wherever. He stands at the median, they say, smiling and gripping his wish. That's him. That's* El Negro Buenavista, *the man who is hungry. The people crank up their tunes and give a look around. That's the man I told you about, the one with a million stories.*

It used to be that I didn't ask for coins. Yes, it used to be that things were different. I was an army man, strong, made something out of nothing when I had to. That was a million years ago it seems. But I'm the same. Only I'm older now and it burns when I urinate. I came here from the capital when the landmines forced us out. My wife, Carmen, was taken from us like that. The people here, they don't understand. But that's no fault of theirs. Nobody understands anybody anymore. They sit comfortably in their vehicles, avoiding me, disapproving of my lowly form. I see them. And only now and then do they listen or make eyes with me. His teeth are rotten like his penmanship they think or say to themselves. But sometimes they listen and some wave. Only the regulars do that. Then maybe they give me the coins that jiggle in my pocket like keys and I buy bread. When someone signals to me I walk over, extend a weathered hand, receive a coin or maybe two or three. Bless you, fine sir, I say. They drive off, humming a chorus and breathing manufactured air. In the distance, the mountains tower, the trees rest at attention. Carmencita, how the children call for you.

Back in the capital, the stowaway children, they sniff glue. I'd see them all the time way back when. They have nothing constructive to do, these little ones. Each day they march the streets looking for the proper thrill. They smash car windows; they chuck stones at buses on the way to the airport; they play ball in traffic, beg for change. And the glue to sniff is always there. Mostly they steal it from school, sometimes in bulk. Sometimes in exchange for labor or sexual favors. Once, I got a boy put in jail for sniffing glue. It's the only way to stop him, I said to myself. He didn't remain there long. He went back to the street and got himself stabbed. This is what the children do in the capital; they sniff glue from paper bags and die somewhere. Señor Buenavista, they used to say. Give us money for food. But I never did. I knew the glue had killed their appetite and they'd only use the money to feed their habit.

There he is, the people like to say now. El Negro Buenavista; the man with a billion stories.

WHEN WE RETURNED HOME, the three of us knew we'd tapped into our calling. The urge to travel and the confidence that we were carrying out some grander purpose weighed on us. We were, in our view, helping to connect people with their maker. Nothing else seemed more crucial, or urgent. We anticipated that in time everything would bloom and catch fire. But we didn't know what to do next, or how to explain all of this to anyone.

The days flowed at their ordinary pace. There were classes to attend and time clocks to punch. Soon enough we received another invitation from the missions group, this time to tour South Africa, all paid for once again. Our mothers had legitimate reservations, but we convinced them that this was providence. If not us, then who would go in our place? we asked. Two weeks later, we set off on a journey that promised to keep us out a month, in Swaziland, Soweto, and Cape Town.

It wasn't long before I was deep in my first crisis of faith. While the wonder that surrounded us was truly insurmountable, so too was the atrocity. We spent days in squatter camps, saw AIDS eating away at the bodies of children, and heard detailed stories about village witch doctors who raped infant girls because they believed it would cure their disease. I concluded that God was not at all present in the physical world, though I dared not say it aloud. At night, I would hear sick children belting songs of praise with great passion, their faces radiating with a peace that surpassed my understanding. Their zeal for life made me feel rotten and undeserving.

The weeks blended one into the other. We logged miles; we packed out stadiums and university auditoriums. I was supposed to be on a high. All the while I couldn't stop wondering where God was. On our last weekend in False Bay, the heaviness culminated in me having a nervous breakdown alone in my hotel room.

After South Africa, we were asked to join the organization full-time. Only now we would have to pay our own way. We agreed; we left college, sold cars, quit jobs and girlfriends, designed merchandise to sell, and received tax deductible financial support from generous donors who believed in our efforts. We found ourselves messengers committed to taking the Word to the far reaches of the earth. I was a tortured soul through it all, pulled this way and that by bouts of tenacious faith and crippling doubt.

Travel broadened my scope of a tangled world. It showed me that kids everywhere are similarly affected by the breaking down of the family. The young people I met were confounded and drawn easily to madness. It seemed few of them had thought to question whether their being abandoned had helped fuel their rage and depression. In Latin America, I felt like I was among my people. They were all houses on fire, moved to action by any bright bone of an idea. They slept around, partied themselves numb, and tussled with outsiders. I learned of their vast dreams, their fears, their complicated home lives. Some of them trusted me with reprehensible secrets. But no matter how reckless any of them were, and regardless of how vile their speech, it only fed my hatred toward their fathers. While we were separated psychologically and by the specificity of our upbringings, we were also very much the same. We were young and we were lost. The only thing that made sense was our hunger, and the hope that it might one day open a path to somewhere we wanted to be.

Part II

The Becoming

If the game shakes me or breaks me, I hope it makes me . . .

We run amok like headless birds, toiling in uncertain times. Storms and quakes displacing families; politics threatening to divide. Frenzy consuming our world. We're stick figures, clay people in the grand scheme; in God's big dream that, you can argue, went to hell eons ago. Still, there's the business of living to attend to. There's the working, the making love. The playing and the praying. It's the small miracles that, in their subdued charm, make up a life. It's more than just the last fifteen minutes of the movie; the death, the proposal.

The small miracles do the heavy lifting. They get us through. Like a friend passing along the perfect book or song just as you were going mad; like the many rivers hidden in plain sight beneath London, invisible threads binding the city.

Cappadonna's verse on "Winter Warz." I can't be the first to believe it was the result of him being possessed by something not of this planet. "Gut you like a blunt and reconstruct your design."

Or watching someone fasten sneakers on a barefoot woman in a crowded park. Catching all green lights when you're running late for an airport pickup. The small miracles soften the blows of the harsh business of living. I read recently that no two snowflakes are identical. The whole dance begins when water molecules slow and settle into order, freezing into crystals of varying shapes. It's beautiful to think about. Like J Dilla's beat for "Fall in Love," with its dizzying piano loop. Or Caravaggio's The Beheading of Saint John the Baptist, *a shrewd and singular display of death and human cruelty.*

Of course, there's when I pull up to the drive-thru at the burger joint to find that the patron ahead of me paid for my meal. Did they know that the only thing coming between me and total bliss was a Double Double Animal Style? Did they realize, before I myself had, that I'd forgotten my wallet and they were the precipitator of a minor miracle? I like to think so.

I think of long shots. I think of canceled plans. The plans you were looking forward to but, perhaps suddenly, don't sound as fly as decent whiskey and Miles Davis's Kind of Blue *on vinyl. Then the text comes: Got caught up, can we reschedule? Yes, you reply, grateful to the high heavens for friends who are doing bold and necessary work.*

Everyday bursts of magic.

Grains of sand under a microscope, each reflecting the biology of the place from where they were taken. The tight grasp of a newborn baby's miniature fingers. How about Kanye West humbly proclaiming "I just want to be remembered" in Paper *magazine juxtaposed with his other loftier claims: "I am a God* and I am Warhol. I am the number one most impactful artist of our generation. I am Shakespeare in the flesh. Walt Disney. Nike. Google."

No sane person without a kind of spiritual agency has the gall to speak this way unless it holds some truth. It was the Vietnamese Buddhist monk Thich Nhat Hanh who claimed:

"People usually consider walking on water or in thin air a miracle. But there's much more. I think the real miracle is not to walk either on water or in thin air, but to walk on earth. Every day we are engaged in a miracle which we don't even recognize: a blue sky, white clouds, green leaves, the black, curious eyes of a child—our own two eyes."

It is true that we are more than the misery thrust upon our minds and bodies; it is true that we are more than the scars left by fires we did not cause; and it is also true that what happens to us is not necessarily what defines us. But if the monster inside goes unchecked long enough, old haunts can fester, like disease.

I kept on with church in those early days because it spurred new ideas. The sermons and old hymns exposed me to language I'd never encountered. It all promised, from what I could gather, a new way to be. For so long my head had felt like a small prison. And while God often felt synonymous with danger, a burgeoning spiritual imagination was there to combat any fear. I hurled Scripture at this fear and waited. Despite having little to show for myself in the way of material, I knew I was in process. I was becoming.

SUMMER 2002. Bright days, hot as all hell. Confusion. Penning rhymes galore. Submitting poems to the *New Yorker*. Reading rejection letters for poems I submitted to the *New Yorker*. Devouring the works of Latin-American writers whose work I'd discovered on my travels. Julio Cortázar, Julia Alvarez, Mario Vargas Llosa. Thinking about the friends I'd made in Colombia. Making songs, sending production references to Chewy. Wishing I could hit the blunt, guilt-free. Trying to imagine what the future might hold. The events of 9/11 had shaken us up, and no one wanted to set foot near an airport. We were scheduled to embark on our final missionary tour in less than two months. I was dead broke and needed a job something fierce.

I thought about that late-summer morning often. 9/11 will forever be remembered as one of the most harrowing days in the history of America and the world. But it was also supposed to be a momentous day in music. I recall that Tuesday with great clarity. A light wind wisped through the trees—tall palms and lushly landscaped hedges showed out like the stuff of postcards. City types moved about the busy Miami streets, hunting café con leche, heading to work or class. Gray steam rose from sewer lines and traffic was the usual mayhem. The weather was finally beginning to cool some. Just barely, but enough that many of us had extra swagger in our step. But the cooling weather was only part of the thing. Jay-Z, Bob Dylan, Mariah Carey, and Fabolous, then a promising newcomer, all had released albums. Borders and Sam Goody were stocked with product, anticipating a big release day. To single out Jay's contribution: *The Blueprint,* his sixth studio album in that many years, provoked high expectations. It featured breakout contributions by unknowns Kanye West and Just Blaze; it had stellar singles. Its soulful production and dexterous lyricism cemented Jay as one of the best to ever do it. At 8:46 a.m. the focus shifted when American Airlines Flight 11 crashed into the North Tower of the World Trade Center. Chaos and panic took precedence over everything, and pop music was no exception. Tours were postponed and television appearances canceled, including the 2nd Annual Latin Grammy Awards, which were slated for that night at the Shrine Auditorium in Los Angeles. A week after the attacks, music sales fell by 5 percent. Radio stations made the switch to all-news coverage, and attention was fixed on trying to make sense of what had happened. Callers shared their stories of grief; money was raised for the families of victims. In the weeks and months that followed, musicians would mobilize to help assuage some of the deep suffering being felt in communities around the country. Once again, the healing power of music and art would play a vital role in American culture. Having visited so many places, sometimes for several months at a time, I knew that music connected people better than anything. From run-down villages in Soweto to Slovakia to an old Baptist church in Crown Heights. Music could unite and bring comfort. And for a while, it would bond people together during tragedy.

We'd been nomads for just under two years, bouncing from one continent to the next, spreading the good Word. We sacrificed holidays with our families, missed birthdays. We kissed dating goodbye, a requirement made by the head of the mission's board, to focus on the work at hand. But we were living the dream—performing our tunes around the world—so it didn't seem like an unreasonable sacrifice. That's not to say we weren't horny devils with ravenous sexual appetites, because of course. We told ourselves we were growing as men, and as thinkers; that the many miles trekked were broadening our worldview, giving us new layers and helping to prepare us for the main stage. Though nobody back home could fathom what our eyes had seen, we were making noise in many of the towns we ran through. Occasionally, the praise bordered on the strange. In Dyurtyuli, a small Russian town in the Republic of Bashkortostan, our fame had spread like mad. So much so that on one red morning we were interrogated by the KGB as a crowd formed around us on a busy square. When they couldn't find any fault, they sent us on our way. Adults forged our signatures on battered soccer balls; kids with disposable cameras peddled photos they'd taken of us to their schoolmates. Naturally, Konata's sold for the highest dollar, as most of the kids had never seen a black person in the flesh. They were fascinated by him. I was fascinated by their boldness.

TIME WAS SLIPPING and I'd applied everywhere, tried everything from retail to food delivery and telemarketing. Weeks flew by and nothing. Me and the boys were recording daily, and with a clear sense of purpose. The plan was that we would complete an album before heading to the United Kingdom for six weeks, our last foray as sexually deprived missionaries. Chewy would have the project mixed and mastered by the time we returned. After that, we figured, it would be on like popcorn. Having paid our dues on an international level, we'd attract high-powered executives and make lucrative deals. We'd grace Big Tigger's booth on *Rap City*; MTV would start playing music videos again. That was our vague sense of what success might look like.

With a month remaining before our trip, UPS called. For weeks, I'd bombarded their office with emails and follow-up calls. "I'm hardworking and a team player," I'd informed the receptionist, who unbeknownst to me had zero involvement in the company's hiring process. "My commitment to excellence is very much in line with the values held by the United Parcel Service," I told her. She said she'd pass along my messages, and to please not call again. Since they'd cut it so close, I considered not accepting the job out of respect. But when the woman explained the position—sorting packages by zip code and destination for $9.50 an hour—I accepted. The schedule was 4 a.m to 9 a.m., Monday to Friday. The situation was ideal since I'd have the rest of the day to write verses and concentrate on invading the industry. I asked her if I'd get to wear one of those slick brown shirts, which I'd always loved, and the woman said, "No. Package Sorters wear their regular clothes."

On the way to work in the mornings, the roads empty and quiet, I'd kick up the radio to ramp myself up. The "Flava in Ya Ear" remix always seemed fitting, mostly because of Biggie's part. I rapped along passionately, laughed at my stupid life as I echoed his verbal assaults: "You're mad 'cause my style you're admiring / Don't be mad, UPS is hiring." I'd stumble into the warehouse and push through my shift, hardly talking to anyone, groggy and half-alive.

I saw Tomás now and then around the way. He was getting

high marks at Broward College and making more paper at the bank than men twice our age. "I'm thinking about taking up real estate," he told me one night when we bumped into each other at the Aventura Mall. "The bank salary is decent, but I'm trying to elevate more," he said. He was pushing a new ride; he had on new Timberlands. I was happy to see Tomás shine, but part of me was envious. The sense of control he had over his destiny baffled me. He knew where he wanted to be and how to get there. I had dreams, no doubt, but I pursued them like an artist drifting in the wind; pulled every which way by circumstance, rarely plotting steps to really blow the roof off my plans. Tomás offered to get me an interview at his branch, if I wanted it. "We're brothers, man, just say the word," he told me. I was appreciative but also slightly embarrassed by his assumption that I needed help, even though I did. I told him about my travels, of which he knew the gist, and how I was preparing to head out again. Scotland and England, I said, aiming to impress. He congratulated me on the *interesting* things I was doing, but admitted to not understanding it all.

I was moving against the current and rationale of my old environment, doing things the old crew never would have imagined. From attending services regularly to helping lead revivals in far-off places. "It's just ill," Tomás said, finally. "Like, why?" I could sympathize with his reluctance, but to me it was like trying to explain love. No matter how hard you try to articulate it, you always fall short of its true essence. Believe me, I tried. I gave him books, I issued proclamations like a street-corner evangelist hoping to show his comrade the way. He just wouldn't bite. While Tomás couldn't grasp the message, it was the method that didn't surprise him. "I always knew you'd be on some rap shit," he said. "You're the best poet I know." That night I lay in bed, repeating his words aloud to try and feel them in my chest. *You're the best poet I know.*

One thing I always had was a muse. Mostly it was some girl I was infatuated with. It seemed like everywhere I went, I found someone new to crush on, someone whose natural charm kept me interested. When I wasn't in love, I found it difficult to write. But that was rare, because in school there was always someone with an energy I found attractive. Some of them I courted briefly, others I admired from a distance. In my new life on the road, I couldn't act on romantic feelings—this was especially brutal when the feelings were reciprocated—because of the strict no-dating policy I'd agreed to. In Honduras, it was Amy from California. In Poland, it was our translator Magda. In Russia, I fell for a girl named Noel who had a nose ring and a dry wit about her. I was sure this last jaunt to the UK would be no different.

Drake: "Landmark of the muses that inspired the music."

I listened to a lot of LL then. James Todd was the unequivocal master of the hip-hop love anthem. I started to wonder why I was drawn to certain MCs more than others. And I landed on the notion that some had qualities that I also recognized in myself. I wanted to put these attributes into practice more, in life and in art. Chuck D, for one, was fearless. Everything was analyzed and disputed. I was taken by his audacity when I was young. Nas had helped awaken the observer in me, the brooding poet who was pure at heart but capable of bringing the pain if provoked. The zeal of Cypress Hill's B-Real, like John Leguizamo before him, showed me that Latinos had a major part to play.

THE DAYS DRAGGED ON, and my spell as a package sorter was coming to an end. I managed to save some paper for my trip, and I was antsy to be out. I had oceans to cross and crowds to mesmerize. I wanted to fall in love again.

One morning, I walked into the manager's office after my shift to give notice. I'd intended to finish off the week, if they'd have me. The man, a dusty-looking old-timer who was obsessed with *Walker, Texas Ranger*, wasn't pleased.

"After all that pestering for a chance?" he said, veins bulging from his sunburned neck. "What the hell, man?"

"I'm sorry, sir, it's just something I have to do. But I can stick around until . . ."

"Screw off."

I turned to walk away.

"And leave your key fob at the front desk!"

THE DAY BEFORE MY TRIP TO SCOTLAND, Ma gave me an old black-and-white photo she'd dug up in her closet. "This is one of my favorites," she said, grinning. "Look at those eyes." I'm about two years old, sitting in front of our home in Queens, New York, where I was born. Besides my birth certificate, it's the only proof that I ever lived there. So much of my identity is tied to Miami and Fort Lauderdale, where I came of age. The streets, the bus stops, the corner stores that sold us liquor and smokes when we weren't yet old enough to buy. Memory makes meaning of it all. But this house in the shot, where I'm told I braved my first steps, means nothing to me. It's little more than a blip in forgotten time. And yet somehow, in some blurred sense, it means everything. Whether I recall it or not, whether the moment exists inside or outside the confines of my faulty brain, it *did* happen. I *was* there. In the photo, I'm perched on a small patch of grass, eyes fixed on my great-uncle Pollo, who stands just outside the gate. I'm looking at him enviously, as if I wanted to be where he stood. Somewhere else, someplace just beyond reach. I seemed to always be looking at things from afar; always sitting on the periphery of my own life.

THE SCOTTISH COUNTRYSIDE has some of the most captivating views— rolling hills, wild marshlands, and mountain peaks. And the medieval castles, which have largely stayed the same since they were built in the Middle Ages, are easy to come by. They're quaint and they tower over deep moats overlooking cities and commanding respect. In Glasgow, we stayed in a nine-story dormitory made of red sandstone. It sat on a narrow winding road and was owned by the Anglican church that was hosting our group for the summer. We had all come from different parts of the U.S., ten wide-eyed youths united by both the burden of our message and the weight of our own insecurities. One morning, after our team had finished our devotional time, I retreated to my room. Part of me wanted to hang back and steal away with Rheagan, this girl from the Midwest who had a smile that slayed me and a pixie cut like Winona Ryder in the nineties. They'd all gone down to the basement, where a Ping-Pong table featured prominently next to the office of a local parish priest.

I had a few hours to kill before we'd roam the streets looking for university students to invite to the night's event. I lay down on the bed, staring up at the ceiling, my mind running laps. Then, a song popped into my head. I reached into my suitcase, where I kept my stash, and took out Tupac's *Me Against the World*. I went to "So Many Tears," the rapper's heartfelt spout on death and longing. I hadn't listened to it in years but now it called out. But not for any reason you might consider obvious.

Tupac: "Disillusioned lately, I've been really wanting babies / So I could see a part of me that wasn't always shady."

For reasons I couldn't fully comprehend, I'd recently settled on the idea that I wanted kids. A slew of them. I didn't have a job, nor did I own a credit card or know how to balance a budget. Yet I knew I wanted to procreate. I'd been fantasizing about fatherhood like I'd fantasized about becoming a distinguished MC or poet. I couldn't explain the sudden desire. I imagined coaching my son's basketball team and enjoying late-night chats with my daughter. Before I knew it, I was scrawling dozens of potential names for my hypothetical children in a notebook. This extensive list—one for boys and one for girls—was broken up by letter; A names, B names, and so on. Why I wanted to send my DNA into tomorrow, who could know.

On most days, we busied ourselves leading assemblies at high schools and colleges across the city. We'd engage random students at parks and hand them flyers advertising the concert we held at the end of each week. That's where we melted faces; that's when I felt most alive.

One day after we broke for lunch, I decided to share with our team leader Johnny what had been on my mind, about wanting to be a dad. I'm not sure why I felt the need to disclose the information—I suspect it was my way of trying to make sense of it—but there I was. Johnny was gracious and kind, but I regretted the decision almost immediately. My words rolled out like a twisted tangle of nonsense. "Well, that's something," he said. We laughed, and I told him I wasn't in any rush, but that the idea had been pressing on me. "I think it's great," he said, in a reassuring tone. "I've just never heard anyone your age sound so certain about it." He told me that he and his wife had been trying to have a baby for years, but there were complications. They didn't know what it was. They'd tried all kinds of medical procedures and nothing would stick. "But we're still holding on to hope," Johnny said. I felt awful for bringing it up, considering how much pain the couple—who I found out years later ended up with six kids—had endured. But that night, on his recommendation, I brought everything to God. I don't recall much of what I said, but I fell facedown in that tiny room in West Central Scotland.

I'd always found the idea of prayer fascinating. And I loved listening to people present their requests and petitions to God whenever we gathered corporately. For me—someone who'd long pledged allegiance to the religion of hip-hop—prayer was not so different than freestyling. But it was its own kind of creative improvisation: carefully chosen words, praise reports like songs, and sometimes pissed-off pronouncements concerning the evils of our bankrupt world. The work of Tupac, to me, was every bit as prophetic as the blood-soaked fiction of Flannery O'Connor. Both required a level of dedicated craftsmanship, and rhythm; a language that lives and breathes and connects. Like prayer.

After Johnny's charge, I took to studying the spiritual discipline more diligently. I read books on prayer, I asked kids from different faiths and denominations—from Muslims to Seventh-day Adventists—how they went about it. There's no secret formula, I was told. You just talk to God. It was helpful, but it always felt juvenile to ask.

One night after we'd gotten back from a rally, the Sadness hit me. A song, a random thought or memory; the smallest thing could trigger it. Konata noticed that something was up, but when he probed, I lied and said everything was copacetic. He knew I wasn't being forthright—by now we were best friends and could see through each other's facades—but he decided not to pursue the matter right then. But when the rest of the team had turned in, Konata and I went to the basement for some Ping-Pong. And there, he asked again: What's the deal? This time I wouldn't hold back. I told him how lost I'd felt, and how many of my old haunts had come back with a vengeance. For hours, we sat in the office of the priest, jabbering about our lives and our music; we cried, we interceded for our fathers. We determined to figure out our next moves together.

All the prayer talk led me back to DMX, Goodie Mob, and Scarface, MCs who wrestled with spiritual matters on wax. Over the next several weeks, I prayed more than I ever had.

Life can be a trip. One moment you're in school eating free lunch with a band of outsiders and the next you're in Scotland asking Jesus for a wife. I never saw any relationship that made marriage seem like an attractive option. They nearly all crumbled; there was no blueprint. Over time, I grew indifferent to the concept. In hip-hop, where we received so much of our teaching, it was seldom discussed. And why would it be? Most of my idols were bombastic twenty-somethings with a propensity for honey dips, gold, and life experience. Monogamy? Please. But there was something even more absurd than the fact that I wanted marriage at twenty-one. Shortly after I started wondering about whom I might get together with down the line, I saw her face in my mind, clear as morning.

Try to imagine for just a moment how ludicrous this is. Twenty-one years old. No career prospects. No savings. No dice. The fact that so much was beyond my grasp, and that I clearly had no clue where my life was headed, made me the opposite of marriage material. Still, you want what you want, however frivolous that makes you.

SLOWLY, Danny began to drift from the group. Now and again he'd casually mention pursuing a career in acting. We entertained his interest and offered up nurturing words when it came up. It became more and more obvious that his musical drive was waning. I saw the light in his eyes when he went on about his favorite films, about so-and-so's performance and its effect on him. "It's a difficult field to break into," I remember him saying once. "But I'm not afraid of that." If anything, I thought, he could become a decent critic. It was clear that Danny's role as a member of a rap foursome now felt more like a burden to him than a joy. It had nothing to do with our friendship—we were tight as ever—it was merely a question of being an adult at a fork in the road; of dedicating years to something only to realize that you want something else. Now that our season as world travelers was coming to an end, we could each do as we chose. We called a meeting and, after a difficult but necessary conversation, decided that when we hit American soil again, the group would be a trio. There was something else, too: I knew that when it came time to tour in earnest, Chewy would not be able to swing it and still maintain a fruitful marriage. So eventually we'd be down to two. But Konata and I both shared an obsession with making it, and that journey was one we understood to be a marathon.

Summer had about dissolved, and Rheagan and I had formed a close bond. We'd stay up late after everyone had gone to bed, laughing, quoting obscure films, and trading stories about our families back home. We agreed to stay in touch after we settled back into our lives. Those last few days together in England reconfirmed what was already known to me; that one day she would love me back, and that we would, as it were, become one. True, I was never much good at relationships. Mostly due to lack of experience. Plus, I was notorious for always jonesing on girls who were spoken for. Like the one I took to prom—and I use "took" loosely because she scooped your boy up in her Honda Civic—I was sprung on her for over a year. That her boyfriend let her go to prom with someone he'd never met told me that he was a stone-cold sucker. Or maybe he was just more secure than me and didn't see my dancing with his girl to "Thong Song" as a threat.

THE PASSAGE OF TIME carries constant reminders of our fleeting desires. Dreams wane and new ones spring up. I was, in every sense, becoming. And my ambition colored my brightest days. It dawned on me that nearly all of my heroes, as they were becoming more and more themselves, had, like me, an obsession with being extraordinary. I wondered: Were we trying to level up on our fathers? Was this endless striving all in the name of restitution? The ones I looked to for guidance came across so steady and self-assured. What were they venturing to prove? Almost all were in their twenties and likely just as unsure of their capabilities as me. They had so much to lose, and such hefty claims to live up to. I'm the dopest, the hardest. "I tongue kiss a piranha, electrocute a barracuda," boasted LL. Jeru claimed his rap could snap your sacroiliac. Sure, the bulk of it was simple street hyperbole. From the outside, though, these rappers were singular miracles. Each was his own brand of crazy, wise, terrifying, stylish, blunt, inspiring, brutal, and loud. Looking back, I know so much of it was fear.

7

BY THE TIME I HIT TWENTY-TWO, I already felt ancient. In my short life, I'd brushed up against things that seemed to add a density to my years. Even my poems, dreadful as they were, had this air of agedness. Like I was some patriarch who'd seen too much and some days wanted nothing more than to watch the hours dissipate through clouds of Newport smoke.

One day I heard a radio commercial advertising an upcoming parenting conference. It was being held at a massive church whose lead pastor was a known star. In the mid-1980s, this pastor had found religion and left behind a life of drugs, debauchery, and positions in several Las Vegas casinos. It wasn't a particularly exceptional story, save the fact that years later he was overseeing one of the largest and fastest-growing congregations in the United States. The spot touted the event as a must-attend session for new parents all the way up to parents with college-age children. Suffice to say that I—a childless college dropout who worked in a warehouse stocking shelves and did rap shows on the weekends—was not exactly the target. That night, I RSVP'd through the website. Who's going to know? I thought. It's not like fools have to mosey around wearing badges that say Mom or Dad.

When I got to the conference and checked in, the woman at the table handed me a badge that read "DAD" in big, block letters. "Here you go, Dad," she said, with an awkward grin. I humored her, saying how grateful I was that the mother of my child had offered to look after him so I could gain useful tips on the intricacies of child-rearing. I found a seat and looked around nervously, hoping I wouldn't see anyone I knew. Like I was in an XXX store surveying the titles, terrified I might lock eyes with a family friend who had a disturbing fetish. The chances were slim, but you could never be too sure. Some people really like porn.

The program featured the names of the evening's speakers. They all seemed smart enough; authors and psychologists with decades of experience in the areas of marriage and family health. One of the names struck me as familiar, but I couldn't quite place it. And I couldn't imagine any other context where I'd have been in the same room as anyone on the program. I took out a pen and paper and waited expectantly.

The first speaker was some kind of youth director and father of three from San Luis Obispo. Using witty illustrations and personal anecdotes, he spoke about the power of positive reinforcement. He was natural and easy when he spoke. The crowd seemed receptive to his talk, especially when he announced that, when it comes to providing encouragement to your child, simply telling them "good job" doesn't always cut it. "Amen, amen!" shouted a lady in the front row to cheers and handclaps. You have to go deeper, the man said. Next was a developmental psychologist and author of a book about getting your kids to cooperate, which was also the topic of her presentation. I took pages of notes. I couldn't help but feel like this parenting thing was a cinch that people complicated unnecessarily. I'm going to be the dopest father ever, I thought. As far as these people knew, I probably already was. I was well dressed and polite, and my presence alone proved that I was open to guidance from the experts. Once the woman finished, we broke for an intermission. There were tables in the lobby filled with drinks and donuts; there were booths for various nonprofits, and energetic interns handing out pamphlets courting potential supporters. Initiatives for ending world hunger, disease prevention, clean water causes; good things all. After a few minutes, people began trickling back inside. I went to my seat, psyched up to soak in more knowledge. The next speaker was introduced, the man whose name I'd recognized. He ambled out to roaring applause, like some beloved host of the late-night talk show variety. Shortly after he ran down his catalogue of accolades, it hit me where I knew him from. It was the same doctor Ma had taken me to way back. The zero-Wu-Tang-lyric-knowing, awful-mustache-having tool shed who'd prescribed me Ritalin when I was shitting the bed in junior high. I sunk in my chair. I couldn't believe he was still on the map dishing out that rubbish. I could have put our history behind us and heard the man out. He had two master's degrees, a successful private practice, and was, apparently, a sought-after lecturer. But I held on to my pettiness, like a prized possession. Anyway, how could I trust someone who'd lied to my face just moments after meeting me? As far as I was concerned, no amount of clout or professional accomplishment could make up for not knowing the lyrics to "C.R.E.A.M." I hoped to make eye contact so I could act out the throat slit gesture, but it didn't happen. It was probably better that way, if you want to know the truth.

I told Rheagan about my time at the conference and she cracked up. "I just love the fact that you went to a parenting seminar," she said, laughing to the point of tears. By then, our relationship had gotten more serious. We'd visited each other in our home states, shared meals with each other's family, made out on her parents' futon. We'd spend hours on the phone going on about whatever; her college courses, my job at the warehouse, the shows Konata and I were doing. "Do you ever miss Danny?" she asked one night. "You guys were so great." Of course I did, I told her. Even though me and Konata were ripping venues and earning our propers on the local scene, for a long time I'd felt that there was something missing in our live set. The magic of three unique personalities feeding off of one another was undeniable, and I wanted that synergy back.

Back when we were first leaving for Eastern Europe, Konata had to break up with his girl Amanda. To eliminate distractions, we were told. While Amanda knew the whole proposition was absurd, she and Konata both agreed to put their relationship on a kind of pause. Or at least claim that they were, so he could have the experience. But when we came home on our short breaks to raise dough, they were inseparable; going to the movies, the beach, doing normal couple things. Amanda was an artist in her own right, and she went by the name Butta, a nickname given to her by her crew back in Pennsylvania. She rapped and sang, and she was damn good at both. While Konata and I were overseas, Amanda had begun to generate some buzz, opening for national artists in clubs from Miami to West Palm. When our commitment was up, Konata and Amanda started to talk about the future. She wanted to get married and he was coming around to the idea. Soon we were doing shows together around Miami, at lounges, nightclubs, and community centers. Anyplace that would have us. Amanda had a commercial sensibility that Konata and I didn't back then. Our sound was straight boom bap, while hers had a pop flare that was more palatable, as they say. She'd hype up the crowd and we'd bring it home. Sometimes it was vice versa. It went on like that a good while, two separate entities that complemented each other, but nothing more.

The days wore on.

Around the time Konata and Amanda had gotten engaged, we three had discussed the possibility of collaborating on something. Nothing about forming a group was mentioned, but the idea intrigued me. What if it went well? Could I see myself in a group with a married couple? Hours in the studio, possibly days and weeks on the road with little time apart? Judging by how much I'd always seen other married couples beef, I wasn't sure forming like Voltron would lead to any desirable outcome. And what if the demands of being in a group put a strain on their bond as husband and wife? I didn't want any part of the blame for a failed marriage. It seemed like a mistake before it even became a topic of discussion. This is to say nothing of the fact that Amanda could be wild difficult, and a real basket case, like me. She was like the sister I never had.

Amanda called and said she'd gotten her hands on some production by a producer she was mentoring. We blocked out some time for me, her, and Konata to vibe at her condo. "Stuff is incredible," she told us. "Wait until you peep his drums." She was right. The kid had a knack for drum patterns and laying down bass lines that made your face turn ugly. I'd only met him once or twice, but this producer had unquestionable star appeal. G-Styles, who later came to be known as GAWVI, was sixteen and a booming talent. On top of that, he was hungry to make moves. Was this the J Dilla to our Slum Village? The Organized Noize to our Outkast? Part of me hoped it was so.

The chemistry between the three of us was intense from the jump. We fed off one another's verses with an almost telepathic energy, like we were one single instrument with varying parts. It felt similar to that first session at Chewy's house years before. And with that, all of my prior concerns disappeared into the ether, vanquishing any doubts I'd had about how it could all pan out. We made two joints and conceptualized a third. The next week, after a long exchange about vision and priorities, we agreed to form a band. Deep down, I wanted to be a writer and traditional poet more than an MC. Rejection letters from magazines and respected journals had convinced me that making music had more promise than the prospect of achieving literary stardom. So I stopped writing poems and stories; I stopped wishing to become the next García Márquez (*The Autumn of the Patriarch* made me want to be a novelist) and concentrated on what was in front of me, which, I deduced, was rap eminence. Though the Sadness came around now and then, contentment again seemed within reach.

ON THE HOME FRONT, Joey was finishing college in Gainesville and was shacked up with a girl on campus; Alejandro was touring and playing drums in a hardcore band; and Andres was the starting quarterback of his high school football team. He was experimenting with hard drugs, and this gave me pause. Though Alejandro and I had smoked our fair share of dope, it seemed our father's proclivity for chasing the higher highs had gotten passed down to the youngest. I can still see Andres's face that first time I picked him up from the station after the cops pulled him over for possession. Something in me broke that night, and I had an inkling this wouldn't be the end of his battle with addiction. In my preoccupation with chasing a dream, I'd managed to let my little brother stray.

Ma and Joe were up and down. When they were good, they were great, but there were times we thought their marriage might not survive. I wanted so badly to break the cycle of weak marriages around me. I sometimes worried that I didn't possess the tools needed to be a good husband. Most of the men I came up around, from my father to my uncles on his side, were cautionary tales. They were playboys who oozed machismo and perpetuated every cliché about Latino manhood. Some were smooth-haired slick-talkers who often viewed women as bodies to be conquered and disposed of later. I understood full well that this stemmed from generations of cultural acceptance, and I hated it. If your mother withstood regular cheating from her man, you will likely approach your own future relationships in one of two ways: either you'll continue the pattern set in motion because it's what you know, or you'll try your damnedest to break the mold. I didn't explicitly judge those who chose the former. Sometimes you have to live and let live. But as I got older, I wanted to do my part to shift perspectives. Of course, it didn't help that Latino men have always been painted with such broad strokes on television and in films. For the most part, that still hasn't changed. But I wanted to challenge the idea that we're only one way, because no group is. In some sense, I was the opposite of cats like Domingo who, in high school, juggled two and three fine girls at a time. Sometimes I wished that I wasn't.

I WAS AT the Coral Square Mall when I ran into one of Domingo's old girls, with whom he still kept in touch as friends. She said he was in town and that he wanted to see me. I hadn't heard from him in years, and last I knew he'd been deployed to Iraq or Afghanistan. She slipped me his math and I told her I'd call him later that night.

I couldn't help but feel nervous as I started to dial. I'd always heard stories of people who came back from war, and how they were damaged forever. How the things they'd experienced had marked them for life. But I was happy to hear Domingo's voice, no matter what his state. We laughed some, reminisced about faster times. Like the weekends we got blitzed out of our heads, or when we would tell random honeys they were one in a million. I could feel that he wanted to tell me something, but not over the horn. He would start up and then trail off, lost in thought. After a while, he said his girl needed him. We made plans for him to drop by the house the next day.

Coming up, people always referred to Domingo as the crazy one. Since his mom was always ghost, most of our antics went down at his spot. I had many firsts there. It was where I'd first heard Public Enemy; where I'd seen my first porno film; where I'd first gotten blunted; where I'd first told a girl that I loved her—a shameful episode I must chock up to the moxie given by a 32-ounce bottle of Icehouse. During our heated arguments, I would often tell Ma that I wanted to live at Domingo's, where I'd be free to do as I pleased. "¡Desgraciado!" she would yell. "See if his mom is going to do everything for you like me!"

Domingo walked up looking cock diesel. He was always slim and naturally cut, but now he had a heft that made him look like a certified army badass. He had a disposition about him that was new; the quiet austerity of someone who'd been in the thick of war and come out physically unscathed. The presence of mind of a trained U.S. Army sniper, which he was. The guilt of more breath, second chances, waffles in the morning. He told me about friends of his who'd gotten shot in combat, others who were caught in explosions. Some lost limbs, others their lives. "Sometimes I feel so isolated," he said. Then he told me what I'd assumed he couldn't over the phone: his girl was with child. It was a boy, and they were going to name him Domingo, he said. "I guess it's my way of starting over," he said. I thought it staggering, the passage of years, and how watching compatriots die in front of you could so transform a man. "I'm so ready for this,

Juan," he said. "I know it's going to change things, but me and my girl are ready to start over."

IN MY MIND, there is a dream—no, a nightmare—that persists. I won't pretend to have extracted from it any meaning, because the mind seems to manufacture pointless bits of minutiae to trick us into pulling substance. At any rate, I'm sitting on the bottom bunk of a bed in a cold prison cell, thumbing through stacks of childhood photos. There's Ma, in all her beauty and grace, posing by a mango tree; there's Alejandro, looking up from his coloring book with a persuasive, contrarian smile; and there's Andres, curious, intelligent, holding a newspaper he cannot yet read. My father and I are nowhere to be found. In the dream, I'm bare-chested on that hard bed, anxiously flipping through the dozens of photos, conducting my own private missing persons investigation. But I'm one of the missing and I can't locate myself in the fat pile of memorabilia. Forget me skateboarding at the park; forget me modeling in front of our record player with my Michael Jackson "Beat It" jacket; forget me practicing my Muay Thai kick in a Bruce Lee Kung Fu Suit with matching rubber-sole shoes. I am a vacancy, a who-knows-where. Just as I'm about to erupt in a fit of rage, my father's voice rises and I jump out of bed. "It's OK, mijo," he says. He's lying on the top bunk in the cell we share. He's covered in tattoos, more than I remember him having. His smile is warm and disarming and we talk through the night, laughing and swapping stories. I tell him about my hang-ups and my ambition and my spiritual convictions. He tells me of his. He tells me of the times that he, like my old friend

Monkey, had found God in strange places. Although he admits they are not, in fact, strange, because God inhabits the earth. He tells me of his upbringing, the anger and the joy, the sound and the fury. The weary load of constantly trying to shield siblings from harm. I tell him I understand. He tells me of his fondest memories with my mother, of walking around Central Park, of how deeply they'd cared for each other, and of their first kiss in 1973. He tells me how his onetime mother-in-law had tried desperately to convince Ma not to marry him; how she wept and pleaded, and how everything my grandmother had predicted came true. That Ma would end up raising children on her own because my father's vices would overtake him. He tells me of the great passion he'd once had for sons and daughters and how he told Ma that if she gave him a little girl, he would fill the pool with beer and never leave the house again. He never did get that girl; not from Ma, at least.

The dream ends. And what lingers in my mind are these words: *a passion for sons and daughters.*

Konata and Amanda got married, and six months later Rheagan and I followed suit. Our growing responsibilities slowed the group down some, but we knew that would change in time. Konata and I were punching in at the Art Institute, where we both worked as advisers, and Amanda was a video producer for a major cruise line. We did shows every other week and slowly started posting loosies online. This was when Myspace was popping and artists could foster connections via the Web and spread their art digitally. The more music we released, the more the demand for a project grew. Around 2006, we founded an independent label and released a full album with G-Styles on production. People were talking. Our name was gaining traction. Out-of-state promoters were booking us, fans were dishing out props on message boards. We sensed that something was happening. All the while, the day gig was sucking the life out of us and we wanted out. We figured it was only a matter of time.

Some mutual friends, an older married couple, contacted us one night when we were at the beef patty spot. They extended an invitation for us to tour Puerto Rico. Greg and Essie were program directors at Teen Challenge, an organization that provided rehabilitation services to young people on the streets who were involved in gangs and addicted to drugs. Greg wanted to set up shows for us at colleges and prisons, and all we had to do was rock mics and cold chill. We'd have to take a week off from work, but everything would be paid for; food, lodging. They had tickets for Rheagan and G-Styles, too. Amanda, being Puerto Rican, was stoked for the chance to reconnect with her parents' homeland after not having visited since she was a kid.

Our shows around Bayamón weren't as official as we'd initially thought they would be. We'd basically just set up a sound system and mics in the middle of a neighborhood or park and go at it. People would eventually drift our way and that would be our audience. Some days it was twenty people, other days two hundred. Around this time, Reggaeton was becoming the wave stateside. But on the Island, olvídate. It was all you heard in the streets, and coming out of houses and cars as they sped by. I wasn't sure we were doing much good—it was nothing like the grind of our former travels—but we were having fun. I couldn't wait to explore San Juan on our off day.

When I awoke that morning, everyone was up, playing soccer and drinking coffee in the courtyard. A lady with a hairnet was outside my room-raking leaves, the light drizzle moving down her face like tears. I washed and dressed quickly as the team waited for me in the van that was to take us to Cueva Clara. When we got there, I was astounded. The place was enormous, peaking at four hundred feet from the top of the mountain where natural streams of water flow into the Camuy River, the third largest underground river in the world. I cupped my hands and drank from the stream as water cascaded down the slick rocks. Within the ancient wonder lay corals and lime stones that colonists had discovered on the beaches of Puerto Rico, the island of enchantment. Easily the most striking thing in the cave was the Hall of Skulls, where rock formations resemble the skulls of Indians and witches. The feel was eerie, and dark. Occasional bursts of light intercepted the darkness, illuminating the walkways where we moved about. I took note of something as my mind, given its surroundings, wandered into spiritual themes. Inside the chambers were sparse areas of deep green, and being that only parts of the cave were exposed to sky, life could only grow where the light shined. That'll preach, I thought.

From Cueva Clara, we made our way to Old San Juan. Most of us wanted to grub and sightsee, check out the architecture and walk the cobblestoned streets. Amanda had more in mind. She wanted to see La Perla, a shantytown that runs adjacent to Old San Juan, just down the hill, at the edge of the Atlantic Ocean. The neighborhood is set between the forts of San Cristóbal and El Morro, next to the cemetery of Santa María Magdalena de Pazzis. I didn't know why Amanda was so intent on seeing La Perla. All I knew of the area was that it had a reputation for gangs and crime, like some of the other communities we'd visited over the last week. As we approached the town, Amanda wandered off. I could see the emotion on her face as she peered down at the rickety homes off the shore. It was a place that, according to locals, cops rarely patrolled. The government had practically abandoned it in hopes that residents would evacuate, leaving La Perla open for development. The talk in the streets concerning its dangers seemed overdramatized. While I couldn't speak on it with any authority, I imagined it was like any other city that had sketchy pockets. One of the women walked over to Amanda, who began to cry as she watched the waves crash onto the beach. The whole scene felt strangely cinematic. Noticing my confusion, Konata filled me in on what the moment meant for his wife. La Perla was where Amanda's father Freddie had grown up in the 1960s. All her life, she'd heard stories of its beauty and its lawlessness; of the many things her pops experienced while living there as a child. Madness at every turn, droves of youth left to fend for themselves. When he was old enough to leave, Freddie fled La Perla for the East Coast, finally settling in Harrisburg, Pennsylvania, where Amanda and her brother Wilfredo were born and raised. Seeing where her pops played baseball and swam as a buck provided a deeper context for who he was. I never knew too much about most of my friend's fathers, just disparate details here and there. As time progressed, and as we grew closer and did more life together, I learned a lot about Konata's and Amanda's parents. It seemed important to make those connections between who we were and what our mothers and fathers had survived. I'm reminded of that old saying: *Show me your friends and I'll tell you who you are.*

If we're so much like our friends, and our friends are reflections of their parents, where do the similarities begin and end? In a way, we're each other's shared histories.

JUST OVER A YEAR LATER, I learned that something I'd long fantasized about, something I'd hoped might disrupt and cancel my Sadness altogether, was to come true. There was life growing inside my wife's belly; I was going to be a father. After the initial rush of joy had subsided, after we'd told our families and dear friends and listened to their kudos and their well-wishes, I was alone on our small porch. I thought about my friends, past and present. I thought about every father I'd ever come across in my young life. And I thought about what my father had said in the dream—about his passion for sons and daughters. If he'd truly ever held that passion, in a dream or otherwise, and could still abandon a wife and three boys, who was to say I wouldn't someday do the same? Ma always told me how much of my father she saw in me. My short temper, my propensity toward conflict. Who's to say I wouldn't break under the strain of this brave new world? Would I stumble into the wrong dive and take up with some broad, leaving my family behind to carve their own trail? This is not to say I wasn't thrilled by what I perceived as an answered prayer. But doubt slowly crept into my gut. I carried it around the way my wife clung to joyful anticipation.

On April 13, 2008, our first son was born in our apartment. He was born at home because people like my wife, who were raised in the Midwest, are an odd bunch. Anyhow, home births have been the natural mode of delivery since the dawn of humankind. It took sixteen hours from the time our midwife arrived to the time I cradled my son in my arms. The ordeal was drawn out and frightening in a number of ways. For a few long minutes—due to my wife's bleeding from having torn—I was tormented by the possibility of becoming a single father. Our midwife remained collected throughout the birth. She stitched up my wife and put a stop to my worry. At first, even the thought of a home birth was troubling to me, and now that initial apprehension seemed justified. I, nonetheless, wanted to support this woman in however she was most comfortable expelling a human life from her body, so that's what I did. Frightening as it was, it worked out in the end.

AS I HELD MY SON, in all his blind innocence, questions flowed endlessly in my mind. Was I equipped to train up a child? Were my dreams dead? It sounds foolish now, but then it was both real and daunting. I thought of all the ways I'd managed to wreck my life and how I was now going to jack up this other life who did nothing but be born. This was no small miracle, and it called for no small response on my part. I thought of the words of James Baldwin: "A newborn baby is an extraordinary event."

People love to talk about how parenthood changes you, but it didn't change me much, if you want to know the truth. Surely not in those first months. It just made me more of what I already was: irritable, prone to neurosis, and compulsive about my work. But my ambition was now tied to something outside of my own self. There was new pressure to supersede what was expected of me, to prove the naysayers wrong. To not only scrape by but shine, like a newly minted coin. On the other side of motivation and positive stress was a deep-seated uncertainty. Almost immediately there was this creature that threatened to swallow me whole, like Jaws trying to dismantle my lifeboat. I was Quint descending into the shark's mouth, its cold black eyes beating and its teeth coming down to end me for good. I knew I had to figure out this father business, and soon.

Following a batch of singles that caused our name to bubble across the country, the group released our second project. It was immediately well received, and our audience expanded as a result. This meant more outside opinions, critiques, and getting roped into conversations and debates in which I had little interest. Namely debates concerning the intersection of art and faith. I thought about A Tribe Called Quest's *Beats, Rhymes and Life* and how some fans dismissed it as being too preachy, the result of Q-Tip having converted to Islam. The lesson is that no matter what, you can never win over everyone. In time I learned to block out the detractors. We were high off the massive support we received and the effort we'd put into the work; the late nights spent bickering and toiling over lyrics, titles, and art. It was focused and astute and aimed to, among other things, establish us as a threat to the local underground scene and beyond. Even from a practical standpoint, it was a departure from any normal creative process, for myself especially. I had memorized more than half of my parts while rocking my new son in my arms. Sometimes as he cried, restless and inconsolable, and other times while I fed him a bottle so my wife could have a break. There was no writing in this season. I seldom had a free hand, and I learned to commit sixteen-bar verses and hooks to memory, stacking them line by line in my head.

AS THE DAYS CARRIED ON, the Sadness grew more frequent. Where before my spells of depression were scattered, now they lingered and increased in strength. I'd never heard of men having postpartum depression, but it seemed probable. Little sleep and unfulfilled desires piled on like toxic waste. And though I never confided in anyone about these matters, not even my wife, I often found it difficult to leave bed. I found joy, on better days, in my son's laugh, in writing and recording, making love, and quiet dinners at home. The group began to travel more and more, and in time me and Konata were missing work. An event on a Friday night in Los Angeles or Atlanta meant requesting a day off, sometimes two. Our bosses liked us a good deal and did their best to accommodate our schedule, but they had a business to run, which now and then required us to dedicate a Saturday. The office life was eating away at my soul, and my escape from the daily drudgery could not come soon enough. On some days, it was truly fulfilling, helping art students navigate their career path. At the same time, it could be discouraging on a personal level. I was an adviser who wasn't taking his own advice. I wasn't taking risks. These eighteen- and nineteen-year-olds—aspiring chefs, animators, fashion designers—mostly knew what they wanted. They just needed practical guidance on how to get there. I envied their position. I wasn't much older, but my growing responsibilities didn't afford me the luxury of dropping everything to pursue my call, like I once did. And it was, in our eyes, just that: a calling. Taking note of our increasingly hectic concert schedule, the staff started placing bets on how much longer me and Konata would remain in our positions. "You two are going places," they would say. "It's obvious." But I was careful to not seem overly anxious in their presence. It felt safer that way.

I WAS IN MY OFFICE killing time online, sour that things weren't moving swiftly enough for my liking. I also felt that I was going mad, obsessing over my dissatisfaction with the state of the world. While the election of Barack Obama seemed like an clear step forward, things were infinitely more complicated. All week I'd been following the events unfolding in Venezuela. The suffering and injustice taking place there was beyond troubling, and it seemed far from over. I thought about Tomás and his family in Caracas; I thought about an uncle of mine who lived but a few miles from the Colombia-Venezuela border; I thought about forgotten children begging for bread in the street. It all made me very uneasy. I also felt distanced from its immediate repercussions. I was angry that millions of people were suffering at the hands of the powerful, yet I was powerless to do anything. What else can you do in those moments but scream and call out to a heaven you may or may not believe in to intervene? While reading some of the news reports, I came across an advertisement for the *No Mas Chávez* march that was scheduled in Miami for that evening. My interest was piqued. I saw that similar demonstrations opposing the totalitarian leader had been slated around the world: Boston, New York, Italy, Toronto. I decided that I wanted to take part, if only in the capacity of an observer. By this time, Tomás had moved to New York to start a real estate firm. I gathered he would be with me in spirit.

The rain began to fall as protesters stood outside the Torch of Friendship armed with flags and colorful signs. Cars passed blaring Spanish hip-hop; drivers honked their horns and shouted as they zipped by. "¡Sí a la liberta! ¡No a la violencia!" they bellowed. Yes to freedom! No to violence! I saw fathers and sons, mothers and their daughters. Families united by a common and measured exasperation. The crowd was made up mostly of South Americans, all who lived in Miami-Dade and Broward Counties. I walked around asking questions, playing the journalist. One protester, a man who was there with his young son, told me he was there to, in his words, protest the shameful atrocities happening in his country. He wanted to demonstrate for his son that he should always fight against whatever threatens to break him, be it a single enemy or a corrupt regime. "It's all I have to give," the man said, and they left, walking down the wet sidewalk clutching hands. For years, the Venezuelan people had been enduring through hunger, extreme poverty, and mind control. Censorship had taken over all media outlets, from news publications to radio stations. Two years earlier, in 2007, Radio Caracas Television had been cut off the air, leading to widespread controversy. The upheaval called into question the role of government and the need to preserve journalistic integrity. Having always held a deep love and respect for graffiti, I was drawn to the movement of political art in Venezuela and its ability to draw attention to the disenfranchised. I saw it in magazines and on the Internet. But the movement of pro-Chávez street art had also been seeing steady growth, confirming, to me, that propaganda was thriving. So while there were many artists making provocative works, the voice of those who presumably favored the president was louder and more thunderous. Given the government's control over the messaging, I wondered how much of these pro-Chávez pieces I'd come across were actually commissioned by the government itself.

I was glad to stand in solidarity with the people, my people. There outside the Torch of Friendship, I was reminded that there was always a fight, a struggle.

FOR WEEKS, my mind could not shake the image of the man and his son. The man's words had felt like a lesson in the kind of parenting that interested me. The kind of parenting that taught sons and daughters about the need to fight back; the kind of parenting that might result in children who were not just accessories or blockheads on which to project our own pain and bitterness, but global citizens who challenged the system and what it stands for. Fresh desire entered into me like air. The thought of that man and his precocious boy blazed in me, and the posture of my heart was altered for the better.

A year and change later, we dropped our third album. It sold well by our standards, and was our first album to chart on *Billboard*. The group reached a level we'd never touched. We'd signed a distribution deal for the record and it proved to be a wise move. It helped us secure placements on television and radio, and our booking fee tripled. I was mostly in good spirits, but the load I carried could feel burdensome at times. Shortly after my wife gave birth to our second son, Konata and Amanda welcomed a daughter.

Two kids meant a more demanding season of life. It meant double the work, double the screams and flailing arms requiring our attention. And a heavier diaper bag full of random things to keep them entertained. I wondered how much more I could carry on my shoulders.

In time, we attracted the attention of a respected manager who was hype about the prospect of signing us to his management company. He had industry connections and was certain he could help open the floodgates. He talked a sweet game and we were sold on his grand vision, his associations and his influence. Konata and I knew that if we signed, it would be impossible to stay at the Institute. We had kids to clothe and feed, so the decision, while on the surface cut-and-dry, wasn't so simple. I wanted assurance that everything would get cracking, but there are no guarantees in the music industry. Things are unpredictable. This disturbed me, but I knew the score. Meeting after meeting, week after week, phone conferences and hypotheticals: we decided that this was our shot. While there was no assurance that our decision would bring about the hoped for prosperity, the chance was ours to take. We were all in.

Konata and I handed in our notice to leave our post of four years. Amanda had left hers some weeks before. Our parents had their concerns, as did our in-laws, but we convinced them there was no other way. We were willing to risk failure for an objective that felt close enough to touch. "Just remember," Ma said, "you have two kids and a wife." As if somehow I'd managed to overlook that fact. I hadn't forgotten. If anything, I wanted to show my sons what it looks like to go after everything you want in this life.

Talib Kweli: "Teach them the game, so they know they position."

We secured office space and converted the four-hundred-square-foot nook into a recording studio. We spent our days working and taking calls with our management and booking agency. It wasn't glamorous, but we'd learned long ago not to despise humble beginnings. We were running a small business and holding three to four concerts a month at first. Our new lives as independent recording artists seemed to be taking shape, and everyone was holding up their end of the deal. Then things started to slow down. Events got canceled; promoters pulled out due to a sudden lack of resources. Months of promise and now the money was drying up. Just like that. We looked to our manager, who was just as baffled as we were. After falling behind on my rent for two consecutive months, I knew I had to either beg for my job back or ask my wife's father for a loan. I hadn't felt this low in years. Shortly after risking my family's financial security to become a professional touring artist, I wanted to die. My passion began to wane and my marriage was in a sorry place. "Sooner or later we all need help," my father-in-law said to me one night over the phone. He said he'd overnight a check for $1700 and not to worry. That night I fell asleep on the bathroom floor, exhausted and downtrodden. I'd failed everyone: my wife, my sons, and myself.

I'd felt like a failure before, but the heaviness of this ordeal was almost too much. I legitimately wondered if there was something the matter with me, something that prevented the stars in the cosmos from aligning so that I could get ahead. Maybe I should give university another go, I thought. Maybe I could find a decent school willing to accept me for my charm and look past the information on my transcripts.

AFTER SEVERAL UNSUCCESSFUL ATTEMPTS at securing another day gig, our manager called. Universal was offering us a distribution contract for a new record and it was time to buckle down. The same week, a close friend of ours who was well off insisted on investing a large sum of money that would enable us to work with a team of decorated producers. We tried our best to reject his bonkers proposal, but our friend wouldn't hear of it. He and his wife had discussed it, and there was nothing we could do to break up their plans. Even though the good news was rolling in, there was still the present to fret about. We needed shows that paid well, and we needed them fast. The summer touring season was approaching, and we knew it would put us in a fair place. We scraped by until then. By another stroke of luck, I was commissioned by a local arts and culture magazine to write a biweekly restaurant column. It didn't pay much, but it was something. Then it was New York, San Diego, Philadelphia, spot dates in the Midwest. We performed at festivals and well-attended conventions. Still, a light autumn itinerary was in the back of my mind. I told our manager he needed to figure it out quickly. One day while we were in the studio, he sent us a message. *I have good news*, he wrote. *Give me a call.*

"ARE YOU SITTING DOWN?" he asked, as we huddled together in our tiny space.

"Jeff, what is it?"

"Are y'all ready to play the Mercedes-Benz Superdome in New Orleans next month?"

"Where the Saints play?" I asked.

"I just got the offer."

"Where the Saints play?"

We flew out to New Orleans with our drummer the day before the Superdome event. I could scarcely believe it. I'd already gotten my check, so I was soaring. Bills paid, birds flying high. We hung around in our hotel for a while before we hit Bourbon Street in the French Quarter, famished. Colorful restaurants made the streets pop with luster. Music roared from systems. Lil Wayne and Mystikal were crowd favorites. Later our driver took us around to explore the city. Seven years earlier, Hurricane Katrina had barreled through the region, leaving destruction and death in its wake. Many lives were lost in the storm, and others lost everything they owned. I remembered watching the news from Miami, seeing the displaced, everyone desperate for an outstretched hand. Mothers and fathers looking frantically for their children. I was no stranger to catastrophic disasters, like Andrew, but Katrina was something else. As we made our way around town, it became evident that New Orleans was still recovering from the beating it had taken. There were sinkholes and severe damage to roads and infrastructure. But the city was still booming. Radiance filled the people everywhere we went.

Show time.

The noise outside the green room was deafening. This was it. The Mercedes-Benz Superdome. Earlier that night, I'd called up Joe to seek his counsel. I was nervous and thought he might share a word that would offer some perspective. "Just take it all in," he said. "Not everyone gets this chance, and you may never get it again." That was all I needed.

Our drummer Pedro was posted up at his kit. The stage lights were off; I could hear our intro video playing and feel the anticipation of the crowd. Pedro texted us just as we were preparing to run out on stage. His message: *this is insane.*

Take it all in, I said to myself, repeating Joe's words.

As the music started, the lights came on. And there we were, standing in front of 35,000 screaming people. The magnitude of it all chilled my blood. We did the damn thing, worked the crowd like the seasoned performers we were. I'd have been surprised if even 500 attendees knew who we were, but it didn't matter. We won everyone over with each passing moment, their fists pumping in unison like a sea of allies. Cameramen followed us as we pranced about the massive platform, projecting our movements on the jumbotron I'd seen a million times before on television. It was a high like I'd never felt. And just like that, it was over.

IT WAS OVER AND, of course, I was still the same man I'd always been. I couldn't revel in the adrenaline rush for too long. I wouldn't allow it. I was keenly aware that while the high was exceptional, it was exactly that: a high. A bright moment from which I had to move on. The future was still checkered with uncertainty. Time was still a train, and it was still closing in.

NOT VERY MUCH LATER, Universal was pressuring us to hand in what we'd promised. There'd been hiccups along the way that always disrupted our progress—most of them factors outside of our control—so the process had been entirely sporadic. We had to complete the record, and quickly.

Once again, I was tapped out. My wife considered returning to work, but after running the math, we determined that all the money she'd earn would go straight to the cost of daycare. Nothing made sense. At night, I quarreled with God and stepped out to smoke cigarettes and interrogate His good will.

After we turned in our project to the label, I was broken and jaded. Like a responsible young man, I made the decision to return to work. I endeavored to put an end to our financial hardships, and to my wife's anxiety over never having enough of anything to go around. All it took was a quick Google search and I found a gig close by, writing SEO-friendly copy for a large moving company. Still, I felt defeated. Every night, I scowled at my reflection and reminded myself what a wreck I'd become. But I had a paycheck at the end of every week that I could depend on. I could stand before my wife and my sons and know that I dared to give them a better life, even it wasn't the way I'd pictured it. But what about the future? I wondered. And what would I make of this impulse to create? It was time to start writing again. I dug up old notebooks filled with stories and poems that were mostly awful. I began to distance myself emotionally from the dream of being a successful musician. Motivation had been choked out. Maybe I didn't want to do this anymore, I thought. I couldn't trust my own feelings.

My brothers were also in seasons of transition. They were getting married and becoming fathers; they were thinking about their careers and about what they might make of themselves. Like me, they were trying to negotiate a season of life for which they were never prepared.

In a strange sequence of events, Konata got hired in the sales department at the same moving company where I was working. We did shows on the weekends but for the most part ignored each other during working hours. We loathed every minute spent in that place, and it felt better to hold our heads and quietly earn our bread. Months dissolved into nothingness, pulling me along. The good and the bad, the beautiful and the banal. Paying bills and scribbling on the side; short articles for the *Miami New Times* and other small papers. The process of writing gave me pleasure, and I was pressed by how much I'd missed it. I now had much more to say. Then we found out we were expecting number three, a girl. But *expecting* probably isn't the right word.

Kanye West: "I walked in the crib, got two kids and my baby mama late."

I'd always wanted a daughter, ever since I was an overzealous young artist with a head bursting with plans. I thought again about what my father had said in the old dream. I'd never told my wife about the dream, but one day I said to her jokingly that now that I was getting my girl, I was going to fill the pool with beer and never leave. She reminded me that we didn't have a pool and that my shift started in five minutes.

To support the release of our most marketed album to date, shows were being booked and our team was scheduling video shoots and press events. This meant that I would have to ditch the office life for a second time. I had a comfortable amount of savings stored up, but I'd been down this road before. Fear enveloped my mind. Quitting was easy to rationalize in some ways, but nearly impossible in others. On one hand, I had a third kid on the way. Though the gig at the moving company was essentially a dead end, it helped meet our basic needs. So was the energy spent trying to make moves over the last year all in vain? I asked myself. Was the investment of time and money a total waste? Or was there something better waiting on the other side of this doubt? All I knew was that dreams don't keep the lights on.

ON RELEASE DAY, Konata and I were at work. We paced up and down the drab halls, livid that we were still toiling in that godforsaken place that treated employees like slime. On the bright side, the group's itinerary was filling up. We were booked solid for the next couple months. The money I would make for these shows was significantly more than my scant salary. But before I had the opportunity to let the boss in on my plans, I was relieved of my duties. Our department of three was informed that the company was ceasing our roles in the weeks to come. That was the end of that. No job, and a third child on the way.

My expectations this time around—even with a support team boosting our clout—were modest. I began to shed my illusions and come to grips with the fact that I was owed nothing. I refused to go about life as though it were any different. The short of it is, things didn't pop off the way many had presumed they would. There were bright spots: we did a gang of shows, joints hit radio, we licensed music to major networks. None of it, while it certainly helped in the short term, could justify what it was costing me. I stuck it out a hint longer, but in the end, it wasn't worth the heartache my steady traveling had caused on the home front. Like me, my wife antici- pated that things would work out. She often believed it even more than me. But my passion for the grind of it, just like my marriage, was on life support. I was on the brink of losing my best friend. Our hearts were growing colder toward each other, and there was a heaviness that loomed over our home, like the air of death hovering over the bed of a terminal patient. I'd become more irritable, and my fuse was short as ever. The constant need to shove off to make ends meet; the pressure that comes with having small children with growing appetites. Anyone who's ever stepped out of their safety zone in order to be heard, or to try to make something they con- sider important, understands. But fatherhood was my truest call- ing; a calling that, while arduous in its own right, was, for me, more urgent than anything I could set out to accomplish. Still, all that we'd suffered over the last years, the shouting matches and the bit- ter nights, had brought our marriage to the ground. I accepted that the only way to salvage the relationship was to move. We packed the truck, said our goodbyes, and headed two thousand miles northwest to Missouri, where my in-laws lived. We'd found a house with a big yard and cheap rent. I landed an editing gig that allowed me to work remotely. I resolved to do what I'd always wanted more than anything. I was going to try to be a writer. Which is to say that

I was going to be myself, truly. I, no less, was a husband and father first, and everything else that might be used to describe me now came second.

IN A NEW CITY, I hit the ground running, possessed by a vision. I'd wake when it was still black as pitch and plug away with staunch discipline. Then I'd drop off the boys at school and spend the remainder of the morning and early afternoon pitching and filing freelance assignments. From my desk I would gaze out the window, drinking low-priced coffee and forgetting to eat. It was everything I ever wanted: creative independence. There was no democratic process to consider, no managers and agents to depend on to close deals. It was myself alone with my ideas and a blank document. There were no friends and no distractions. There was no need to leave my family for days or weeks to scrape by. I began writing criticism and contributing articles to national magazines. Checks were coming in, and for the first time in what felt like forever, I was reasonably satisfied with how things were evolving. Given my constant working and overall lack of human interaction, it wouldn't be long before I was downcast again. Truth was, all my life I'd been leaving, running from something. Traveling always gave me a sense of purpose, as if being gone meant that I was someplace conducting necessary business. But it didn't fix me, and I couldn't escape the blank page, real or figurative. It was time to face this fact, and to be fully present as a family man, and the writer I desperately wanted to be.

8

BIBLICAL WISDOM tells me children are like arrows.

I thought about that portion of Old Testament text a good deal the first time I read it. To me it was, and still is, a feast of language. My kids were very young when we began our life in the Midwest, but I could see the fight in them. And my chest would ache when I watched them act out film sequences—dressed the part—every bit of stern in their flips and front kicks off our sofa. "Like arrows in the hands of a warrior are children born in one's youth."

In ancient times, the men stood on guard at the city gates. Prepared to handle any threat, these protectors, these men, kept alert through the watches of the night. With their sons, they remained shoulder to shoulder, each breath drawn in defense of the other, in defense of everyone within the gates. That picture constantly swirled around in my head. I liked what it said about solidarity, and about the deep heart of a father. The imagery, too; and how it reminded me we're made from the stuff of war and desire. I especially liked that it made me think of my own boys, who were glad to protect anything if given the word.

WHEN WE FOUND OUT we were expecting our fourth, it was something to grapple with. The news came in the midst of some dark days. I processed it alone, the way I'd been processing everything since arriving in Missouri. I had my work, but I was starved for connection—I had not one single acquaintance outside of the family—and I didn't know quite how to remedy it. That first winter was brutal on my Florida bones. But I mostly embraced the changing of the seasons, the outdoors. In Miami, we have sublime beaches and palms, but it's mainly skyscrapers, bodegas, and urban development. All wonderful things, no doubt, only not on the level of the Ozarks, with its rivers and bluffs and mammoth caves. I remember seeing God one gray morning, posted on a bench at Sequiota Park. He was taller than I'd remembered. But I hadn't paid much attention to Him for some time.

Chance the Rapper: "I speak to God in public."

When I thought about us adding another to the brood, at first all I could think about was myself. I wondered how I'd manage with all these arrows. I questioned if I was man enough, really man enough, to handle all that fatherhood was demanding of me. It made me consider how we view masculinity in our culture, and the great change we've all opted into undertaking. Things took a turn after the Industrial Revolution, to be sure. Men began to focus more on their careers and making money, leaving women to fill the gaps. These days, men are changing diapers and packing lunches at impressive speeds. The roles are interchangeable, as they always should have been. But still, trepidation kicked in.

THE MORE I BEGAN to investigate my own depression, the more I was forced to face the history of mental illness in my family. By now I recognize that I've made mention of the Sadness many times. Though I did not plan to make it a part of what I'd intended to do here—which was to chronicle my journey to manhood and fatherhood and what it has meant to me as an artist—I've come to accept that it would be disingenuous to leave out these details which make me who I am. That is, who my family is. On both sides, my mother's and my father's, a fair share have either tried to end their lives or succeeded in doing so. Cousins, my uncle, my great-grandfather, my grandfather, who, along with my grandmother, was always a source of strength and stability. The revelation of my grandfather's attempted suicides shook me harder than any other. So I asked questions, I drew timelines. I tried to understand the root of his suffering and, in some way, correlate it to my own to find any detectable pattern. But even at my lowest points, I'd never, not once, thought of taking my own life. I didn't judge those who had, because the details of our personal wars with our minds are complex. The sort of darkness that, I imagine, must torment a person in their final moments is something I find easy to sympathize with. It is conceivable to understand that sometimes we want nothing more than to free ourselves from the burden of living. When people—especially those who never made much effort to see the full picture—used words like "selfish" to describe those who'd died by their own hand, I always saw it as an oversim-plification. Just maneuvering from one day to the next can prove difficult, and everyone is given their own mess to figure their way through.

OF MY GRANDFATHER'S TWO suicide attempts, one came about after he'd lost his dry cleaning business. I was in grade school at the time. It wasn't the first time he'd lost everything.

My grandfather once had a small finca in southwest Colombia, with chickens, pigs, and cows. After he'd secured a contract with a local market, he began to supply them with meat. He also sold fruits and vegetables to a handful of vendors around the city. But one day when he was out, a nearby river overflowed and swal-lowed up most of his livestock. Upon hearing the news, he rushed home to the brutal sight of dozens of dead chickens and pigs floating downstream. He took his canoe and tried to salvage what he could, but it was useless. His farm was through. Long days and nights followed. My grandfather took on odd jobs here and there until he'd saved enough to move with his wife and kids to the United States.

He had battled depression since his early teens; since after his own father bit a bullet in the family van. Being that he was the sec-ond oldest of five children—two boys and three girls—my grand-father was forced to get a job fairly young. When that didn't bring in enough income, he got a second job. His father had left behind some money, but as my grandfather later learned, it was only suf-ficient to send one of the boys off to school. And his mother chose the oldest boy as it was assumed that he was the brighter of the two. My grandfather, though he carried that resentment with him, proceeded to make his own path. He worked hard and put himself through school, performing menial tasks to cover his expenses. He eventually became an accountant and found himself carrying the entire family, including his brother who did nothing with the opportunity he'd been given to learn a trade. But something in my grandfather had broken. And over the years, my grandmother struggled with him through his Sadness, which almost always made itself known after he'd had a few drinks. After he had disappeared once for almost a full day, everyone started to assume the worst. He was in a bad state after losing this first venture in the United States, and the house was on edge. *It's fine,* my grandmother would tell him. *We'll get through this.* But he couldn't get past what he saw as his second great catastrophe, which was the end of the dry cleaning business.

Around 2 a.m., Ma and my grandmother were notified that an officer had found him. He was sitting in his car in the empty parking lot of a shopping center in Lauderhill. When they arrived, Ma approached the vehicle and saw my grandfather's head resting on the steering wheel. There was a gun next to him on the passenger's seat, and he was gripping the handle in his fist. Ma begged him to open the door. *What are you doing?* she screamed over and over. Finally, after several minutes of pleading, he gave in and fell into Ma's arms. They checked my grandfather into the hospital to run tests and provide him with much needed therapy. While he was away getting treated, my grandmother found the suicide note he'd left days earlier. In it, he begged for forgiveness and went on about his love for the family and the guilt he felt for having let them down. He told my grandmother that he adored her, but that she'd be better off without him. After spending ten days in the hospital, my grandfather showed signs of improvement and they sent him home. He began painting again and singing the tango at our house parties. To this day, my late grandfather's paintings, which are spread out across the family, are some of the most mind-blowing I've ever seen. Deep down, he was always sore that his responsibilities never afforded him the chance to pursue his art with abandon. I felt a similar fear for a long time.

AT THE HEIGHT OF MY DESPAIR, I took a trip to San Diego for a wedding. Considering the state of my own marriage, the thought of watching two lovebirds embark on one of civilization's most ancient traditions struck me to the core. But I couldn't miss it. One of my dearest homies was tying the knot, and I was honored to be among those standing by his side for the ceremony. I thought of the many conversations we'd had together over the years. His joys, his apprehensions; his strong desire to be a good man, husband, and future father. By now, it was impossible not to consider every flourishing relationship through the lens of my own regret. I realize the self-centeredness at the heart of that statement, but it was my cross to bear. I was regretful of the ways in which I'd fallen short over the years. Faithful, but not always present. Expecting patience but slow to reciprocate it to my bride. Truth is, I had so much to offer my friend; wisdom I'd picked up along the way, warning signs he should look out for. But I felt I was in no condition to offer counsel, and I feared my heavy words might somehow quench the excitement in his eyes. So I drank instead.

The ceremony itself was nothing short of a dream. Sunshine, the bluest waters, and palms towering behind us like set pieces. The weather was California-perfect and the air thick with cheer and promise. My friend looked handsome and confident and his bride could not have been more beautiful. Then came the reception, and madness ensued. Better to spare the details, but I'll say that I knocked back about five too many Manhattans and made an entire fool of myself. I chased cars in the parking lot and ran my jibs to strangers hanging around the marina. I mention this merely to illustrate my utter recklessness during this time. The next morning, I had to phone my friend's mother and beg forgiveness for my antics. I was sick and ashamed; I couldn't wait to get home and back to my work.

I'D LONG BEEN AN AVID READER, but now I began to read more widely and vigorously. I versed myself in everything from Russian classics to the Spanish playwrights and socialist literature; writers whose names and works permeated the films of the French New Wave. I would listen to Mos Def or Raekwon while reading Clarice Lispector, and consume the pages of Haruki Murakami while Nas and Mobb Deep extolled Queensbridge through the speakers. To me, it was all the same. Gateways to elsewhere. They helped me see the world more clearly. Before long, I was reviewing books by international authors, interviewing rappers, and writing biographical sketches. After my review of a novel by a little-known Japanese author went viral, sales for the book began to shoot up. The independent publisher New Directions, which has been around since 1936, had never had one of their titles become a *New York Times* best seller. "Only a few people seemed interested in reviewing it, but one of those was Juan Vidal, a reviewer for NPR Books," the publicity director for New Directions told the *Times*. "It took everyone fantastically by surprise here. We didn't think it would do this well. It climbed up and up . . . and all because of a single review." The credit was the author's, but I couldn't help but feel validated. I felt like my words mattered now, in a way they never had before. It was the loneliest and yet most productive period of my life; a welcome change from years of touring and the mania that came with it.

On the road, I lived constantly in the shadow of my father's cheating. Temptation came in no small measure. Whether at a stadium or smoke-filled nightclub, there was always at least one shorty down to slip out the back and get familiar. But having Amanda in the group served as a kind of buffer. She learned to observe closely when people were getting too attached to me or her husband—women who were drawn to men with a microphone and a platform. She'd spot it quick and politely intervene. Nothing ever happened, but had Amanda not been around, things would likely have played out differently. I might have gone the way of my father and uncles, whose capacity to resist temptation was about as thin as my patience for their remorse.

In my new life, the days were far less tantalizing. But they were meaningful in their own way. To me, nothing was more exhilarating than getting the words right on the page; nothing sweeter than putting down my truth—my enthusiasms, my ideas about life and culture and hip-hop—and casting it like a net out at sea. Some I sent off to get published, others I stashed away in folders. I was groping toward purpose, toward what felt like my fullest self. My daughter was too young, but the boys saw it. When they were smaller, I'd rock them back and forth while committing raps to memory. Now I recited long form essays just to see the looks on their faces.

Raekwon: "Me and the RZA connect."

Soon after an article I'd written on the Wu-Tang Clan's RZA got published, I was contacted by Adisa Banjoko, founder of the Hip-Hop Chess Federation. He told me that he and RZA were taken by the piece and that he'd be in Missouri the following month, at the World Chess Hall of Fame in St. Louis. He was organizing a host of events in partnership with the nonprofit and asked if I might want to join him. There might be a story, he said. I said that I'd be happy to tag along, but that it was two hours away from where I currently lived, in Springfield. "RZA is going to be there," he said.

I went silent.

"That's why I'm reaching out," he said. "We're going to be speaking in schools and detention centers, teaching young people about hip-hop and chess."

THE SCHEDULED EVENTS would be happening just outside of Ferguson, where two months earlier eighteen-year-old Michael Brown had been murdered by police officer Darren Wilson. Intrigued at the prospect of getting to shadow one of my longest standing heroes for a day or two, I immediately sent word to my editor. "I have to go," I told him. He agreed; I had to go.

Soon, I was making my way up I-44 E toward St. Louis in a rental.

For several weeks, the protests and the unrest in the city had dominated the national news cycle. There was anger, frustration; businesses were destroyed by fire and cars burned to the ground. Talking heads called them riots, but we knew it was an uprising. To know the difference was to be paying attention. Every night cops threatened the multitudes with weapons and tear gas. People felt that they weren't being heard or, for that matter, valued. An uprising felt like the only possible response to having been silenced and dejected for so long. So much of our nation's hatred and racism was being brought to the forefront, like it had been so many times before. Brown's death triggered a nationwide debate concerning, among other things, Ferguson's largely white police force and the systematic prejudices that had been prevalent in the community even prior to the murder. It was reported that in 88 percent of the cases in which the department used violent force, it was against African-Americans. This visit by RZA wouldn't fix the problem, but in the minds of the event's organizers, it might offer some glimmer of hope to the surrounding communities who needed it.

When I arrived at 4652 Maryland Avenue, Adisa was there to greet me. He was tall and friendly, and seemed genuinely happy to make my acquaintance. He gave me a tour of the World Chess

Hall of Fame—a large red brick building with bluish-gray trim and big windows. He presented me to some of the organization's leadership—"This is Juan from *Vibe* magazine"—and I walked around the two-story structure, enthralled. There were galleries and there was a gift shop hawking souvenirs and antique collectibles. Ceramic chess sets, trophies, and plaques of the Hall of Fame members lined the walls. There was custom-made furniture that had belonged to American chess grandmaster Bobby Fischer. It was a fantasy world of art, chess, and philosophy.

"RZA will be here tomorrow morning," Adisa said. I nodded and thanked him again for the invitation.

He walked me across the street to what they called the Chess House, a gorgeous mansion where the WCHOF puts up honored guests visiting from out of town. I freshened up and a group of us walked to a small dive for drinks and to discuss the weekend's plans. While there, we got word of another murder that had just occurred. Exactly two months removed from the death of Michael Brown, another black boy had been killed by an off-duty police officer. We anxiously checked our phones, texting and scouring social media for details on what exactly had gone down in the nearby neighborhood of Shaw. My chest burned with anger at the thought of another boy's parents losing a son. I thought of all the times I'd seen Brown's parents wailing on television. What the hell was going on? We ordered another round and called it a night, the city dark and muffled around us. A city on pins and needles.

RZA was posted up center stage, wearing all black and addressing a room of more than three hundred high school students at the Demetrious Johnson Charitable Foundation. He was talking chess, martial arts, and hip-hop, his three greatest loves. Sitting across from Adisa, RZA was dropping science and fielding questions from the anxious teenagers. "Listen," he said. "The people with brain power are the ones that will always rule the world."

With St. Louis on the verge of implosion, the youth in the packed auditorium were desperate for something they could hold; an antidote that might help them make sense of the violence and negativity that had their city under a microscope. At a point, RZA stood up and unleashed an impassioned speech on what he called the 12 Jewels of Life: Knowledge, Wisdom, Understanding, Freedom, Justice, Equality, Food, Clothing, Shelter, Love, Peace, and Happiness. He unpacked each principle with a fervor that would excite even the coldest skeptic. And everything was tied seamlessly to chess, both as a discipline and as a metaphor for purposeful living.

Later that day, at the St. Louis County Juvenile Detention Center, RZA's approach was even more direct. "We have to start thinking more analytically," he told the inmates, a few dozen teens who were all slated to be back out on the streets soon. "Y'all are in here for not controlling your energy," RZA said. While most of them weren't hip to RZA's musical legacy, they recognized him from some of his television and film roles.

"Oh, man, we just watched *The Man with the Iron Fists!*" one of them yelled.

"You were in the one with Denzel, you were in *American Gangster,*" shot another.

"How rich are you, how many cars?"

RZA satisfied some of their curiosities before going into a testimony about the ways in which chess, martial arts, and hip-hop had helped him sharpen his life skills and carve a unique path to success.

"In the beginning, I saw my Wu-Tang brothers as chess pieces," RZA said. "I knew all their strengths and they let me be their Abbot. I calculated moves and made nine millionaires. Like y'all, I made some bad choices growing up, but that's in the past."

RZA paused.

"You all got to understand something," he said, inching closer to the feverish crowd who was hanging on his words. "You can't get any of those moments back, but if you spend your time wisely, you can earn more time."

What RZA saw before him, he told me later, was youth in revolt. They'd been let down, abused; many of them were abandoned by their mothers and fathers. But the more RZA spoke, the more engaged and reflective his audience appeared. They believed in him.

BACK AT THE WORLD CHESS HALL OF FAME that evening, a sizable crowd had gathered for a gallery reception presenting the work of local artists and filmmakers united by their love for St. Louis. Heated protests were taking place blocks away, with residents eager to know what was to come of all the violence. The question of whose role it is to serve and protect was thick in the air. Later, after chessboxing with RZA and listening to the Wu's upcoming album, *A Better Tomorrow*, the Abbot and I were left alone on a stoop outside the Chess House. We talked about music and chess and fatherhood. RZA took an interest in my sons and my daughter. How old were they? he asked. What did they like to do? I told him they loved hip-hop and drawing and skateboarding. "Hold them close," RZA said, his trademark lisp cutting through me. "They grow too fast."

Following what I believed to be a perfect weekend—the highlight being my exchanges with RZA—I wanted desperately to do better, to be better. I don't mean to overstate a few brief conversations, but RZA's words and public speeches helped affirm things that had already been bubbling inside me. The need to struggle harder at your vision; the task of properly stewarding the young lives you were given to mold. My call to fatherhood was, by now, fully realized. It was plain that what had been reserved for me was the privilege of stewardship, of leading and caring for sons and daughters. In other words, I was being called upon to help build a better world. A better tomorrow.

I pulled out of St. Louis late the next day feeling brand-new. With no set destination, I cut through side streets and explored the different neighborhoods, burning gas money that I would expense later. Soon, I happened upon a charming European market in Hyde Park. It was surrounded by rows of boarded-up houses. I learned it was a family-run shop that had been serving the community for over seventy-five years. The woman at the register said even Pope John Paul II was a onetime fan, that he'd enjoyed their famous sausage during his time as a cardinal in 1969. I bought some bread and salami and sat outside on the curb to eat.

I was instantly transported; reminded of the many months I'd spent roaming about Poland in my early twenties. The trip had left an indelible impression on me. I remembered wandering the streets and hoping that being there would somehow help me understand Joe better, as his family was from a small town not far from where we stayed. For several months, eight of us stayed in a convent in Lublin, a bustling city southeast of Warsaw. The convent was run by a group of bewilderingly happy nuns, some of whose names and faces I still remembered well. They'd pace around busily in their black habits, sometimes beating their tambourines and playing electric guitar in the shadowy halls of the convent. These were eccentric nuns; they were like no nuns I'd ever seen or heard of. For dinner, they'd serve us stuffed cabbage and borscht; they'd tell us stories about the bands they'd played in before they entered the ministry full-time. On our off-days, Konata, Danny, and I would sniff around Old Town eating pierogis and living as though we had life all figured out. But something about being in that old Polish sausage shop in St. Louis triggered another memory: I recalled the exchange I'd had with my father after I'd returned home from Poland. I was telling him about the country I came to love so much, my stepfather Joe's country. More specifically, I was telling him about my visit to Majdanek, the concentration camp nestled on the outskirts of Lublin. Originally constructed to hold POWs, Majdanek later became a killing center during the Holocaust. Our guide had showed us around the many crematoriums and execution stations. I ambled around the barracks, where Nazi soldiers used Zyklon B, the cyanide-based pesticide with which they killed over a million people in gas chambers in Majdanek and Auschwitz. I marveled at the Majdanek Memorial, which held the ashes of countless camp victims. I surveyed the storage depots carrying piles of old shoes, photographs, suitcases, eyeglasses, toothbrushes, and prayer shawls. All around me was the memory of cold, hard death; of men, women, and children whose lives were snatched from them. I thought a lot about the children who'd died in these death camps. I saw their possessions, their hairbrushes and tiny hats. Children were a vulnerable lot in the era of the Holocaust. Day after day, the Nazis killed scores of unwanted children, some of them immediately after birth. Every moment spent in Majdanek was a new kind of unsettling. I remembered thinking about my future children, who I prayed would never die before I did. My father asked how it all made me feel and I told him that it angered me. I told him that part of me wished I'd never seen some of the things I had throughout my life. I told him how much I hated it that people suffered. I told him I couldn't wait to be a father someday. Then I made up an excuse for needing to hang up the telephone.

When I got home from St. Louis, I committed to delving more into my past, organizing jumbled memories like rooms in a large house. Maybe I was doing research for a book I would later write; maybe I just got a rush out of torturing myself. That much wasn't clear. But I was thinking of my legacy, and what the whole of my existence might later mean for my children.

Balancing the demands of creative work and family life is no simple feat. It became an even greater challenge after baby number four came along and straight rocked us. Most of our friends back in Miami had one kid, some of them two. But in the Midwest, it wasn't unheard of to see fathers with five and six rug rats at playgrounds and mall food courts. Or packed out in Suburbans on their way to someplace green. It wasn't so different than the way my parents and grandparents grew up, and many of my friends' parents and grandparents. The older generations, mothers and fathers who hauled around mad kids, had to give up a lot in order to manage. My grandfather couldn't pursue his painting like he'd wanted, and Ma, a single parent with no free time, couldn't become the fashion designer she'd dreamed of becoming as a young girl. Stitching garments for extra cash wasn't exactly the plan. And therein lay one of my greatest fears: that being a father, something I'd always wanted for myself, would require that I give up my quest to become a major artist. In short, to do what I loved. To tell the stories that moved me.

I understood that sometimes you have to forfeit things, to die little deaths. But giving up everything you love always seemed like a path laden with bitterness and resentment. I didn't want to end up crushed inside like my grandfather, whose paintings, had he had the space to bloom as an artist, might have graced the coveted walls of museums from New York to Paris. But times done changed, and we live in an era infinitely more advanced and with greater possibilities. I resolved that instead of forfeiting my hunger, I would work tirelessly to ensure I never had any more regrets. That was an example I wanted to set for my sons and daughter.

While Ma had to forgo certain dreams, there was at least one thing that she didn't give up on. Something she'd always wanted since moving to the United States in her twenties: to become a U.S. citizen. The process proved to be a stressful one but she stuck it out. I remember being eight years old and going with her to the immigration offices, my teeth on edge. Standing around for hours at a time, rooms packed to the full with adults and their rowdy children; the stench of Marlboros and knockoff cologne; the nervous anticipation; loud, broken Spanish echoing off the walls. I devised rhythms and made games for waiting: I looked at everyone's shoes and tried to imagine where they'd been, what roads they'd traveled. In the end, Ma's persistence paid off. She did what she'd promised herself she would do. My father never bothered with it.

AS MY KIDS GREW NEEDIER, I began to see Ma quite differently. I was struck anew by how she'd managed to raise up three boys alone. I always knew she'd endured a world of hurt, and I was mindful to bless her for it. It wasn't until I had a gang of children of my own that I got a clearer picture of the weight she'd carried. I was jolted by it. Her goodness came into full view like a light across the sky. For the many years before Joe put a ring on it, there was no partner around to help ease any of the stress; someone to remind her to mail the utility check; a companion to look after the kids when she was running behind the clock. Despite her boys' waywardness through the years—the drugs, the school suspensions, and the trouble with the law—Ma never fronted or wavered in her love for us. I learned that a mother's love for her sons is a chord not easily broken. Nor is it anything less than a touch of glory on earth.

With this realization came a profound sense of pride in having been raised by a woman; especially *this* woman. Not that I'd have chosen such a road, or what it cost our family. But I was forced to bear witness to the innate capacity of a woman. The capacity to love and forgive and to hold our jagged, imperfect world together. As the oldest son, my relationship with Ma was always different than her relationship with my brothers. There was no favoritism on her part, and each of us was well loved and treated fairly, I submit. Yet there was an unspoken understanding between us. We alone shared the memories of my father's darkest episodes. His cheating, his bullheadedness. We understood that these memories would forever live on in the both us, like tattoos on the mind.

EVERY MAN I'd ever exalted in some way eventually let me down. In word or in deed. Every man except my wife's father.

During that first year in Missouri, my father-in-law was diagnosed with atrial fibrillation, which causes the heart to beat in a fast and irregular rhythm. I learned that in AF, blood pools in the atria and doesn't pump properly in the two lower ventricles, which can result in various complications. "Slow down," the doctors told him. "You'll be better off." They put him on a strict diet, and in time he disposed of his tobacco pipe and cigars, some of his greatest pleasures. We used to smoke Parodis like Clint Eastwood and stare out at the night, sometimes not saying a word. Only the sound of our breath and the trees brushing against the leaves. Before the year was out, my father-in-law would undergo two electrical cardioversions, where they send an electric shock to your heart to reset its pace. Besides being the best man I know, he's also the hardest working. He runs a small college and maintains thirteen acres of land, mowing and planting and chopping down trees for firewood like it's child's play. Everyone knew it killed him to have to scale back on his projects, but he gathered it would only keep him around longer. In all this, he taught me that a real man puts others before himself. He does whatever the cards demand of him. This man was, and is, like no man I've ever known; tender and even-tempered, but capable of fixing a leaky toilet and building you a house with his hands. When he and my mother-in-law would visit us in Miami in the early years, five minutes wouldn't pass before my father-in-law was grabbing at something to repair. He'd jiggle a loose doorknob or hear a funny sound coming from the washing machine and say, "I can fix that if you want." While it wasn't his intention, his offers to fix things always made me feel like an imbecile. As if, because I hadn't done it first, or because I wasn't taught how to fix this or reupholster that, I myself was broken. Damaged. A spaced-out artist in a family of practical Mr. Fix-Its. But once I'd gotten over my bruised ego, I was just grateful for the man he is. For so long, I'd learned to live with minor breaks around the house. Weeks would pass before I'd even notice a squeaky cabinet door or a light flickering in the kitchen. If a towel bar had come unhinged, I'd put my towel somewhere else and keep it moving. While I was never the most fluent, I believe in the poetry of manual labor. I believe in the woodcutter's song, and the shoemaker's. I believe a man in a field taking a hatchet to lumber can be just as poetic as a verse from Kipling, although definitely not as exciting as Ghostface Killah's verse on "Guillotine (Swordz)" where he raps, "You fourteen carat gold slum computer wizard / Tapping inside my rap vein causes blizzards." That's just transcendent.

ONE MORNING, my mother-in-law found her husband lying on the bathroom floor, barely conscious. Some hours before, he'd gotten up to yell at the dog to quit barking but he never returned. He'd blacked out, apparently—had knocked his head on the sink and fallen. Back then they lived out in the woods, surrounded by dirt roads and rolling hills that make me dizzy to think about. The closest hospital was roughly thirty miles away.

When the ambulance arrived, they rushed my father-in-law to the hospital and immediately took him to surgery. After some tests, they discovered a blood clot in his lungs. Fear arose in our hearts. But soon we grew swollen with hope, like he had taught us. The doctor prescribed rest and medication, and my father-in-law slowly recovered. Within a handful of months, he would have a heart attack and get in two serious accidents that nearly took his life. For a long time, he made an art out of cheating death.

FOR ALL OF ITS CHARMS, I couldn't remain in Missouri long. Two years and I was cooked. Not even the low rent and the affable strangers could keep me away from Miami; from our community of friends, the sunshine, and the nonstop movement. By now my marriage was on the up, and we were thriving. Ma was ecstatic to have her grandkids back around making a mess of things.

I paid the bills writing magazine articles and criticism. I went to shows and attended readings and festivals. While I enjoyed reviewing books and conversing with MCs and authors about their work, I started to feel like I was ready to tell my own stories now. As a musician, I'd had the privilege of putting five albums out into the world. My videos had appeared on television, singles got radio spins. No one could erase the memories of the places I'd been and the things I'd seen. But I wanted more than just the memories of a former life. I thought I might finally have something bigger to contribute.

Some night I came across a Samsung ad for Jay-Z's *Magna Carta Holy Grail*. In the spot, Jay is talking to Rick Rubin, who's barefoot and outstretched on a black leather sofa, his bushy white beard bouncing off his chest in angelic fashion. Jay is opening up about his father, and how he never showed him how to be a man, or how to raise a child or treat a woman. After becoming a father, Jay was, as many of us are, struck by the gravity of this new role. Soon came an almost crippling fear of failure. Fear of falling short as a husband and a dad. "I'm lying if I said I wasn't scared," he rapped once. Growing up fatherless left him feeling uncertain and completely ill-prepared. A few years earlier, in 2010, Jay had released his book *Decoded,* which offers a vivid and arresting portrait of his upbringing in the Bedford-Stuyvesant neighborhood of Brooklyn. In the book, Jay breaks down some of his most popular lyrics and details many of the stories that helped fuel his debut album *Reasonable Doubt*. But, and perhaps unsurprisingly, the most affecting parts of the book are the ones in which he describes the fatherless youth who inhabited the drug-infested Marcy Projects, and how finding a creative outlet helped some of them overcome their environment.

"We were kids without fathers," Jay writes, "so we found our fathers on wax and on the streets and in history, and in a way, that was a gift. We got to pick and choose the ancestors who would inspire the world we were going to make for ourselves."

These words left me gasping for air. I felt an intense conviction inside to begin to document my own misadventures, and my own brushes with failure. I started thinking about all the music centered on fatherhood that had resonated with me over the decades. One of the jams that stuck out the most for me was "Away from Me" by Little Brother.

THERE'S NO SENSE in trying to convince anyone that Phonte Coleman, front man of the Foreign Exchange and cofounder of the defunct but underground legendary rap trio Little Brother, should be on every hip-hop heads list of top tier MCs. In this case, it's better to just hope one's taste is good enough to know. To recognize that *The Listening* (2003), *The Minstrel Show* (2005), and *Getback* (2007) are singular masterpieces that have more than stood the test of time. As a rapper and singer, Phonte has long been the voice of the *everyman*, the cat with a family who can make art of even the most common minutiae, illuminating it all on wax with a refreshing candor. From his earliest recordings, he's never shied away from sharing his grievances and personal struggles, from the agony of divorce to his journey as an artist and father. Phonte set himself apart in the early 2000s, establishing a reputation in rap circles as an MC's MC, a poet par excellence. He tackled the complex dynamics between men and women with the wisdom of someone twice his age. It wouldn't be a stretch to assume it's because Phonte became a father fairly young.

"Away from Me" features Phonte and Big Pooh swapping stories of love, loss, and strained relationships. Phonte's verse stands out as he describes the pain and frustration he felt in being separated from his first son while the rapper was trying to make moves early on.

> *Right now it's all about this long distance*
> *All I can do is get along with it, try and be strong with it*

One day I listened to "Away from Me" over and over until I concluded that I needed to speak with Phonte. I told myself it was imperative that I let him know what the track had meant to me, and how so much of it mirrored my own experience. I sent word and a date was set. After a brief introduction, I hit him with an abundance of questions. As expected, Phonte was wise and generous.

On family dynamics:

"In the family unit, a father is the first line of defense. Obviously mothers are incredible, and kids very much need a mom. But a strong house starts with a man. Boys, specifically, need a man to give them a name, to validate them and their masculinity."

Phonte shared anecdotes and cited passages from *Wild at Heart: Discovering the Secret of a Man's Soul* by John Eldredge. I knew the book well and had read it with interest during my years overseas.

On emotional fatherlessness:

"Sometimes grown men, out of their own insecurity, look for women to validate their manhood through sex and relationships. And that can be fatal. Truth is, we need another man to tell us that we're a man when we're young."

On settling into fatherhood:

"I never saw myself as a dad. I just wanted to make music and tour the world. Having a family wasn't even in my thought process, and for a long time I struggled with feeling like that. Eventually, I had to let the guilt go, though. Just because you didn't grow up wanting it doesn't mean you can't be a great father."

On fathering black boys:

"One thing I've realized is that, for black boys, childhood ends at around nine or ten years old. At first you're this lovable little black thing. But as soon as you get some size on you, you're automatically perceived as a threat. These are some of the uncomfortable truths I explain to my boys, to prepare them for the world they live in."

On parenting as an investment:

"This investment doesn't pay off for like another thirty years. That's parenthood. A few years ago me and my pops got to connect. Being a father myself now, it finally helped me understand him more. There are cycles to this, but we don't understand it fully until later."

I understood something of the cycles Phonte was referring to. The way our understanding of our role in the world comes in fits and shifts. From the present making no sense to a sober perspective of things suddenly haunting your every waking moment. Epiphanies. Minor miracles.

As always, I was intent on writing my way through it all. I often didn't know what I thought about anything until I scribbled it down and arrived at a working theory or position I could live with and, if it came to it, defend.

DURING THAT TIME, I would write the bulk of a novella only to toss it in a shoebox filled with random keepsakes from my travels. I wrote a pilot script and became bored of the characters before shelving that, too. Inside me there was an unrelenting desire to arrive at something personal. I wanted to contribute something that might reveal beautiful truths about the human experience. To break my own heart and watch it burn somewhere besides my own chest. It seemed like every other month I'd start a project only to abandon it when it became too difficult to improve upon or complete. I felt like I was giving up time and again. I was haunted, day and night, by my shortcomings, which became more and more pronounced as time slipped. My aspirations were alive and well, but my ability to concentrate for long stretches was growing dull. I was juggling kids, multiple dying projects, bills, bookish notions, old hurts that I knew would never fully fade, and a writer's block—though I shudder at the term—like I'd never encountered. More than anything I wanted to know how other fathers did it. How they balanced making significant work while remaining loving and engaged caretakers. People like Jay-Z and Phonte and RZA had done it, and were continuing to do it. These were fathers who were master jugglers. But it wasn't just them. I looked around and saw so many other fathers who were master jugglers; my friends, and their friends, and their friends' friends. Men who grew up fatherless but who were now shifting the conversation. I wondered if these were the stories I needed to tell. The stories of rap dads who had somehow been overshadowed by those who perpetuated old stereotypes.

ONE REDDISH MORNING, I was standing on the balcony, coffee in hand. Dawn was breaking and the house was motionless and dark.

Outside, the grass was caked in dew and the curbs were washed bone-white from an early downpour. Scrolling through my feed I came across an article citing the many myths surrounding black and brown fathers in America. In it, the writer detailed how, while certain stereotypes still persist in contemporary culture, there's another side that goes underreported.

"If we look at the ground level, black fathers are there all around us. If you come to my block you will see black fathers and husbands celebrating with their wives and spending quality time with their children."

I was reminded of the old Chris Rock bit in which the comedian jokes about people trying to take credit for doing things they're supposed to do. "I take care of my kids!" Rock shouts, as if simply fathering a child qualifies you for a medal of honor. "I ain't never been to jail!" he rails. The point, of course, is that these are things a normal man should never feel the need to boast about. "What do you want, a cookie?" Rock says. "You're not supposed to go to jail, you low-expectation-having motherfucker!"

There's an underlying tension that gives this particular joke an added layer. The truth is, men do want credit. Not a pat on the back for performing their moral duty, but recognition for the fact that they've broken a cycle of fatherlessness in their community, which may go back several generations. One can safely assume that a man who boasts about taking care of his kids came up without a male figure in the home. He did what his father either didn't or couldn't do. This is not to suggest that men should need to be coddled or constantly reaffirmed for their good deeds; that's child's play. The point is that so many boys maneuvered through life without any consistent male presence. So when those boys become fathers, respectable ones that love and provide, they see it fit to celebrate themselves.

While there are issues that must be addressed in communities everywhere, the conversations about the state of fatherhood and what it looks like have remained one-sided for too long. Black and Latino men, in the main, have been almost exclusively associated with drugs, prison, gangs, gun violence, and the like. Rarely do people outside of major metropolitan cities get to see us in the mix, atoning for the masses of culpable men the realm over. Put simply, there are corners of the media that have conditioned people to see the world the way they want them to see it. When people are fed these same images over and over, it robs the exploited of their complex humanity. I thought of the many times I was out and about with my four kids and a stranger would stare at me quizzically. Are those all *your* kids? As if my mere presence seemed to challenge everything they'd ever believed to be true about young Latino fathers.

I took a drink of my coffee and looked out at the street. Someone's pit was barking viciously a few doors down. I watched as some of the early crowd made their way toward the bus stop or to their cars. I thought about all the projects I'd either tucked away or shredded. I had a grip of pending assignments, but I couldn't shake the sense that I needed something more rousing to work toward. After a while, I saw one of my neighbors, a Puerto Rican man in his late twenties, heading toward the pool with his small daughter. He was leading her by the hand slowly and carrying a pink inflatable in his other hand. The little girl was smiling; her quiet joy the result of her father being attentive to her needs. Right then I knew the story that I wanted to tell. The one that had been in me all along. It was the story of the rap dad.

Part III

Future of the Funk

My newfound life made all of me magnified . . .

THE STORY OF MAN AND HIS BROOD is the story of the world itself. Past, present, and future.

In the present, some are taking the old models of fatherhood head-on, our hands and feet in the muck. But as I've spelled out, the jungle from whence I came was light on men who acknowledged their namesake, if they stuck around at all. The divorce rates were staggering, and for some, dejection was our daily bread. In 1988, around the time my folks were calling it quits, the *Palm Beach Post* reported that Miami held the second highest divorce rate in the country. Countless mothers were forced to inherit a seemingly impossible task, working double time simply to get by. My father hadn't kicked the bucket like some of my friends' fathers had, but he just as well could have been dry bones in the ground. I was always trying to measure my loss against theirs.

Out of this sense of desertion, we gravitated to art that helped us process our longing, a hunger that for so long went unnamed.

As an artist, I cannot so much as think about fatherhood without considering some of the material that deals with feelings comparable to those I felt after I became a father. Songs that contextualize very specific emotions over cold drums, and the men who were pressed to reevaluate their positions in a cold world.

In his 2012 track "Glory," Jay-Z reflects on the birth of his daughter Blue Ivy, his first child with wife Beyoncé. Produced by the Neptunes, "Glory" was released on January 9, just two days after Blue was born. From start to finish, it carries a sort of gleeful melancholy that resonates on multiple levels. While it is, in essence, a comment on the exuberant joy attached with welcoming a child, "Glory" is also a note on death and mourning.

Before Blue came along and flipped the script, Beyoncé had suffered a miscarriage. The pain the couple experienced left them fearful of not being able to conceive. The dual purpose of "Glory" is made clear from the outset, and with blazing transparency. "False alarms and false starts," offers Jay, laying the groundwork for what immediately follows: "All made better by the sound of your heart." The second half of the couplet establishes what was, as we come to learn, the most pivotal moment in the rap mogul's life up until then. The moment where all is made right, where the sting of loss is eclipsed by the possibility of new birth. Jay continues in this mode, shining light on the redeeming gift that is Blue and, also, how the child is a composite of her mother and father, yet more still.

The opening bars of the following verse are equally striking as Jay, addressing Blue, touches on the death of his father from liver failure. Jay is signaling here, leading us somewhere but with the intent to shift gears. Instead of dwelling on his father's shortcomings like one might expect him to, Jay breaks left, resolving that deep down his father was a good man. And so: what begins as an indictment of a cheat who walked out on his obligations, ends with a declaration of forgiveness and generosity. But Jay soon directs the focus back to his blessing and how hard it is not to spoil her rotten as she is the child of his destiny. It becomes apparent that this is a man at his most self-actualized. A few more welcome digressions and "Glory" closes the same way that it begins, with the final line of the hook: "My greatest creation was you." This points to something that I, too, came to know as fact. That no matter what I do, and regardless of what I might attain—power, wealth, the esteem of my peers—nothing is quite comparable to the happiness and the terror that comes with siring a child. "Glory" succeeds as it casts aside any traces of bluster and bravado, making room for Jay to unearth lessons that were hard-won yet central to his maturation. And what is the purpose of making art if not to bust open your soul and watch it spill over?

THERE'S NO DENYING that hip-hop is the most dominant cultural force of the last three decades. People like me who were conceived in the early eighties, and others in the mid to late seventies, are part of a generation of hip-hop parents born around the time the culture itself came to be. It's almost inconceivable to think that hip-hop was once dismissed as a passing fad, like stonewashed denim and the sanctity of marriage. Now it informs everything. It's used to market products, rap feuds consistently dominate the social media space, and it made it to the White House on the watch of Barack Obama.

As a buck, I never could have envisioned the places hip-hop would take me. But I was too jaded to forecast much beyond my ruthless environment.

At one time, my deepest distresses came from the lingering threats of my father's enemies, and my own insatiable hunger for meaning. But those were my school years, when I was surrounded by roving misfits and murderous Latin Kings, the lot of us broken and self-obsessed. One of the main questions in my mind now was whether Tomás and Domingo had arrived at similar conclusions about the things that nagged at me. Had they, too, grown past the skewed visions of masculinity displayed by the lion's share of men in our lives? Had they pardoned their fathers like Shawn Carter did his father Adnis Reeves? It wouldn't be unreasonable to assume that they'd disrupted the family cycle; the curse perpetuated by generations of men who sold out their kids for drugs and instant gratification. Considering what we knew about rejection; considering that our eyes were stricken daily by black and brown faces wandering madly without a guide. Who of us wouldn't want to take part in changing that narrative? Now I saw rap dads everywhere with tykes in tow; little ones smoothed out in Air Jordans and clean fitteds, flipping the fashion script. Kids that were hip-hop down to the bone gristle. Their slang; their attitude; how they cut a rug at house parties while the adults discussed the day's mathematics. The counterculture had claimed their parents early on, so for many of these shorties there was hardly any choice. Now we shot hoops and curbed our language, our kids orbiting us like small planets.

Amor.

Much of what Konata and I had learned about love we picked up from raps and from the wounded women in our lives; our mothers and aunts. This meant that as kids we often saw only half the picture. While these women meant well, if we took everything they said as gospel truth, then there were only two types of men in this world. There was the stoic but passionate man working in the yard and the cool pacifist jotting poems about trees in a forest. So what of the men who don't fit either mold? It would be more accurate to say that most men probably occupy a space between both extremes.

For too long, my life was governed solely by my feelings. Like so many boys I knew, I lived by my gut and acted on impulse. I would bang the wall when something demanded a detailed game plan. Games of strategy like chess and Risk evaded me because I was unable to reason two and three moves ahead. I never learned how to calculate my steps. As I grew in age and more was required of me, I thought very much about what it means to be a man. I thought about all the machinery that I lacked, and I thought about the excuses I always made for my deficiencies. Every layer of my consciousness became fixated on determining if I was a man or a fraud.

Around when I first began to study the biblical view of masculinity, the same time that I was reading *Wild at Heart* somewhere in Eastern Europe, I made a lengthy scrawl on a legal pad; a manifesto about what I thought a man should *do* in order to be considered one. I reasoned that a real man raises his own; he toils and provides for those in his care; a man is an upright citizen; he pays his taxes and sets aside his tithes for the house of God. A real man, according to me then, serves others faithfully and makes himself available to be poured out like an offering unto the Lord. The church figured heavily into my definition. Many of the men in that old Pentecostal congregation, predictably, thought it mission-minded to don apparel that featured scripture and have bumper stickers on their rides announcing that "Real Men Love Jesus." But looking back, some of it seems a good deal flat. It's absurd to believe that a man can only qualify as one based on the quality of his performance. What I mean to say is that, while these things are good and honorable, they are not what makes a man a man. If a man so happens to do none of these things—if he chooses to run from his calling like Jonah when he dipped to Nineveh; if he turns his back on his work and his kin; if he rejects his religion—is he not, then, a man? Is the title of man something you gain by adhering to a certain set of behaviors? A man's actions, however good and honorable, cannot possibly be what presupposes his being a man. A man is a man because he says he is.

There's nothing all that original about the rigid codes of masculinity to which I was exposed as a child. In my community, and communities like mine, boys were taught, whether by words or by the actions of the OGs in the neighborhood, that men were a superior lot. We were taught that the more girls you hit and quit, the more of a boss you were. It meant that if you were gay, or behaved as if women were equal to men, you were not a *real* man.

When people think of terms like machismo, naturally, they associate them with Latino men. In fact, a very clear-cut image comes to mind when I hear that term. I think of Razor Ramon and Benny Blanco from the Bronx. But machismo is a patriarchal structure as old as time, a system built on exerting control that has long rejected any veneer of softness in men. It is, in many ways, the antithesis of feminism. Where feminism is, in part, about fairness and contending against a historical oppression of the fairer sex, machismo, like the notion that "Real Men Love Jesus," is about power. It is about supremacy. And hip-hop, for all the positivity the culture has brought, hasn't always been keen on shedding old patriarchal skin. But this is slowly changing, especially as young men continue to become young fathers. This is why "Glory," and other tracks like it, remain necessary. If we engage with them properly, they can move us closer toward truth and beauty.

Common: "Having a child shouldn't have to bring out the man in me."

For a thousand years, I was a boy trying to figure out how to become a man in a country that's become more hostile to people with names like Juan. I recall wishing as a kid that I'd been given a name that was easier to digest, like Tony or Mark. It irked me that my name was somehow difficult for others to negotiate. Challenging, apparently, to pronounce, and so clearly foreign. But that was then. And while I no longer wish that my name was whiter, I'd be lying if I said I didn't wonder what strangers thought of me at first introduction. What did the woman from the insurance company immediately assume about me when I asked for a quote? What does the gentleman at the swanky new restaurant think when I phone to put in a reservation? We all have our biases, but it's never amusing to be on the receiving end.

Not very long ago, my family and I were taking a cross-country road trip to visit with relatives. Our otherwise pleasant trip was interrupted when my Jeep began to shake in the middle of Nowhere, Kentucky. I tried hard not to project any fear onto my wife, and to react calmly. But inside it was another story. There are multiple Americas, and this one just happened to strike fear in me. I was gripped by a sense of alarm and what I considered to be a reasonable distrust of my environment. This was during the height of the 2016 presidential campaign, when the rhetoric surrounding immigration and Latinos on a whole was top of mind. There were large pockets across middle America, and everywhere else, where people freely expressed their hatred for us. At the same time that young black men were being slain in the street by trigger-happy cops, others with names like Juan and Miguel and Guadalupe were getting harassed, beat down, and told to go back to their country. Tensions were thick and I felt the burden of 57 million Latinos inside my veins. The Jeep barely made it into the lot of a Dollar General before it stalled out.

There were a few patrons idling outside, smoking and shooting the shit. I told everyone to stay inside, and I approached the small crowd of scraggly men, the hair on my arms shooting up. "Hello," I said. "Howdy," one of them answered. I decided they were all mechanics, as their hands and clothes were stained black with what looked like motor oil. As a precaution, I introduced myself as John. I didn't think twice about it, like my natural instinct was to shield my family from any possible threat posed by the weight of my name; as if that could protect us. As if these were the sort of people who made assumptions about a person based on what their parents chose to call them. The fact that I'd been deemed racially ambiguous more than once—strangers have fancied me everything from Italian to Middle Eastern—was an oddly comforting thought. That I, a fair-skinned Latino, might pass as non-Hispanic seemed, in a situation as sensitive as this one, like a form of privilege. Except for the fact that it required a kind of erasure of the most basic part of my identity; the most fundamental component in my sense of self; the very thing that over time had grown and spread over me, like skin. "My name is John," I said. "We're just passing through, me and the wife and bambinos over there." I pointed at the squad and they waved, the kids all wide-eyed and clueless. I explained the issue, told them the ride had crapped out unexpectedly. One of the men let out a terrible cough and asked me to pop open the hood. In an instant, three or four of them were hovering over the engine, pulling at tubes and unfastening lids. A man in Dickies overalls went to his truck and came back with a vehicle diagnostic reader. He plugged it into the computer system and waited for it to signal a code. Almost a minute passed and nothing happened. No code. He gave it a few more tries and still nothing. Something was obviously not right. My wife took the kids into the store to stock up on sugar and salt, and I entertained the strangers. "What did you say your name was, fella?" one of them asked. "John," I said again, no wavering in me, whatsoever. "Well, John, I don't know what in Sam Hill is going on."

It was early Sunday evening so the local body shop wasn't open for business. No one could get through to the master grease monkey, who they said would surely be able to figure out the problem. I wondered aloud if perhaps I'd filled up with contaminated fuel along the way. Anything was possible, they told me. I went inside and purchased a bottle of fuel injector cleaner, hoping it would work and put us back on the road. After I spilled every last drop into the tank and turned the key, the thing let out a roar. The crowd erupted in applause; men, women, and children who'd all been invested in this moment for the last hour of their lives. I thanked them for their time—"Adios, amigo," someone offered, confirming that I'd fooled no one—and we drove off, Dilla beats pumping loud beneath a clear sky. I felt like the man; I was myself again. And while I was half-ashamed that this troop of kindhearted Kentuckians had been unfairly judged, the sensible part of me knew it could have gone down differently the next block over.

IN *BETWEEN THE WORLD AND ME* Ta-Nehisi Coates writes that black people love their children with a kind of obsession. I submit that this also rings true of the immigrant Latino community from which I sprang. The fact that so many of us came up with our mothers as our sun, moon, and stars meant we were subjected regularly to their wrath. But I would argue that when Ma took the belt to my backside it was more about intimacy than anything, a way of trying to shield me from outside harm. Those licks, for all the pain they caused, were a window into a parental love that was possessive but well-meaning. For my mother, there was a sense that if she carried out justice herself, if she beat my ass good, it might keep me from paying a higher price for my trespasses elsewhere. No matter how flawed that rationale may have been, a fierce devotion remained at the core. In my family, and in many families like mine, love was a physical act that could border on the cruel.

I was talking to Alejandro—by now a staunch Libertarian with a penchant for debate—about this one day and he got heated. He countered that in no way can a beating ever be rationalized under the guise of love. Alejandro and Andres both have sons, and Alejandro is particularly vocal about his feelings on corporal punishment. It's child abuse, he says. That's all, and that's it. He gets off on passing me articles and statistics that delve into the negative effects of spanking. The mental and emotional damage it can potentially inflict on small children. He doesn't believe it when I tell him those whoopings did me good.

In November of 2008, Barbara Walters interviewed a newly elected President of the United States Barack Obama and First Lady Michelle Obama. America was deeply curious about these two anomalies, and Walters saw it fit to dig into the more intimate details of their relationship and family life. When Walters broached the topic of parenting, she inquired about the couple's approach to disciplining their girls, Malia and Sasha. Obama said, "We don't spank." He and Michelle don't have to resort to hitting, he said, because the girls genuinely dislike disappointing them.

I didn't like disappointing Ma either, but you wouldn't have known it by how often I screwed up and pushed her to the limit.

Barack Obama: "In my first term, I sang Al Green. In my second term, I'm going with Young Jeezy."

Barack Obama is without question the quintessential rap dad.

He is the paragon of how high hip-hop has been elevated and how far it's traveled. From the parks of the Boogie Down to 1600 Pennsylvania Avenue. As the nation's first black president, Obama not only became the apex of black manhood, but also the realization of generations before him. Not to mention he was the first, if not the only, president that many people from the two largest and most powerful minority groups in the U.S., blacks and Latinos, could relate to. As commander in chief, Obama was outspoken about his affinity for MCs like Jay-Z, Lil Wayne, and Kendrick Lamar. Throughout his tenure, Obama quoted rappers in his speeches and made references to songs that inspired him across the pop music spectrum, from "Dirt Off Your Shoulder" to "How Much a Dollar Cost." He bridged the gap between hip-hop and politics; he extended invites for artists to perform and engage in political discussion at the White House; he had private meetings with some of music's most prominent figures, from Chance the Rapper to Andre 3000. In a televised concert that celebrated the opening of the National Museum of African American History and Culture, Obama was seen on camera rapping along to none other than Public Enemy's "Fight the Power."

The closing moments of Obama's final White House Correspondents' Dinner speech in 2016 were nothing short of legendary. It was one of his most defining hip-hop moments, and a fitting capstone to a historical two-term presidency. After a thoughtful and at times witty address, Obama puckers his lips, shoots the audience a peace sign, and says, "Obama out." He drops the mic in classic hip-hop fashion and struts off, the crowd cheering and dazzled by the master orator's closing trick.

IT WAS HIP-HOP THAT SAVED MY LIFE. And it was fatherhood that set it on fire. This bears explaining.

What hip-hop did for me is what it did for millions of heart-wounded kids—it provided, at the very least, the shading of a better life. The soulful samples and confessional bars weren't road maps necessarily, but they helped me conceive a way out. A way out of the hallowed halls of Silver Lakes and the many snares of 10th Court. We walked home minding our business, our heads low and our headphones on—enamored by the sounds of the poets and beat makers ringing in our ears. Their revolutionary words and crisp 808s called to me like signals from another planet.

Music played an instrumental role in helping me navigate not only a path out, but a path forward. If it wasn't for hip-hip, and the value I ascribed to it, it would be impossible to know just how far I'd have settled into the more lamentable aspects of my environment. Forasmuch of a goon as I was, something always kept me from becoming too emotionally invested in harsh crime. I dabbled in mischief like an intermediate chef knowing he would only go so far. I saw in hip-hop, in the art of it, something worth pursuing with tenacity; something like healthy distraction. So I committed to finding my lane. Though there were brief stints dedicated to developing my modest graffiti skills and footwork, it was the words that flowed and came without struggle. The cyphers sharpened my wits and compelled me to feed my vocabulary daily. Only my wordplay could save me from getting ripped to shreds in a lunchroom battle. I read books and scoured the dictionary for ammunition, I listened to stand-up comics who fearlessly engaged the crowd and proved quick on the draw. It seemed fruitless to know a billion words if I couldn't convert them into brutal attacks. I had to break the competition down and render them defenseless, stammering for a rebuttal. I had to make them small, and it had to be clear to everyone within the sound of my voice that I was the victor. There could be no confusion as to my superiority. Instead of joining the stickup kids or depositing all of my energy into intramural sports, I put my soul and mind into the task of taking down all manner of wack MCs. That's why I say that hip-hop saved me.

But fatherhood was its own saving grace. It showed me that the world did not revolve, nor would it ever revolve, around my passions. Fatherhood put an extra battery behind my back, sure. But it became more important to be a consistent presence at home than to chase some spark of momentary glory. It set my world on fire.

I WASN'T ALONE. The more I thought about how hip-hop and parenthood were interconnected in my life, the more I saw that it was the same for countless others. Curiosity enveloped my mind with new degrees of vividness. I wanted to talk to mothers and fathers, hip-hop heads who grew up similarly—and differently—but for whom the culture had filled a similar void. I interviewed rappers and producers, writers and media executives. I scheduled phone calls and lunches, all with the aim to discover my world anew. I went in expecting wise answers and cheat codes, as if life were a Nintendo game that could be hacked. Instead, I found people like me. People who were trying to figure it out as they went. We exchanged experiences and drew from one another's wins and losses. Some shared details that were so intensely personal I questioned why they were being offered so casually. But there's power in making yourself vulnerable. In each conversation, I sensed the collectivity of our lives. The mysterious ways in which our flawed humanity could lighten someone else's burden, if only for the length of time it took to swap a few stories. We were parents who owed everything to the culture that helped give us meaning. And now we were trying to pass it down, everyone in his and her own way. Whether it was our love for trivial things like sneakers and snapbacks or stressing the value of unfettered self-expression, we were teaching it. The information was going forward.

IF I WERE FORCED TO CHOOSE from a swath of favorite MCs, I would put Nas at the very top. I was barely thirteen when a friend put me up on to his seminal album *Illmatic*. "This is that real," he'd said, in a tone that suggested everything that came before it was simply inferior. He was right. But since enough words have already been spent testifying to the singularity of Nas's 1994 debut, I'll resist the temptation to go there. Instead, I want to pivot to "Daughters," a cut from his 2012 album *Life Is Good*.

As the title suggests, it centers on fathers raising up daughters. But where Jay-Z's "Glory," which was released that same year, focuses on Hov's newborn, Nas's "Daughters" details the challenges of fathering a teenage girl. The opening line is enough to put a knot in any man's chest: "I saw my daughter send a letter to some boy her age."

"Daughters" examines the weighty responsibilities of fatherhood while straddling the line between stern and sympathetic. Throughout, Nas fesses up to his own naiveté, exploring themes like teenage sex, the traps of people-pleasing, and the fact that our kids will never be perfect. What prompted "Daughters" was the drama that ensued after his daughter Destiny—who was seventeen at the time—posted a photo of a box of condoms to social media. Of course, the Internet erupted. As critic Jon Caramanica wrote in the *New York Times*, Nas comes across as conflicted between forgiving his daughter her transgressions and indicting himself for not having been a strict enough parent over the years. Appropriately, Nas and his daughter both feature in the music video, which traces Destiny's life from birth to the present. Concerning Destiny's response to the track, Nas later told *Vibe*:

"I think she understands where I was coming from. She can hear me saying that I wasn't always around and I wasn't always the best dad, but I care. And there are a lot of fathers like me. To me, 'Daughters' lets all those fathers out there know, 'Hey, don't end up like me in terms of not being there all the time.' You should really pay attention to the most precious thing in the world. Destiny and I hang out all the time. She never beefs with me about it."

As a father, Nas's words land close to home, hitting me with great force. They make me reflect on my own approach to parenting while bringing complex questions to the surface. Will I succeed at instilling in my daughter a balanced sense of self? Am

I preparing her from a young age to know her worth and conduct herself with the knowledge of that worth? One thing I've noticed is how, as men, we tend to treat our small daughters like delicate princesses, soft as feathers. Over and over again we remind them how beautiful we think they are and how dazzling they look in their new dress. This is fine, of course, and very much needed. Still, we can't deny that our selfie-obsessed culture has conditioned us to prize perception above all. So while it is good and necessary that young girls have their physical appearance affirmed by their fathers, I often wonder if we're raising one-dimensional beings who will someday feel entitled by their warped sense of beauty. Over time, I've become more cognizant about the language I use when affirming my daughter. Beauty is merely one of her attributes, and, I would argue, the least important. I need her to know that, while she is certainly stunning, she is also strong, fast, intelligent, tenacious, and capable of doing anything her brothers do. And not just because I feel the need to say it for my own gratification, but because I believe it. I believe her drive, her fortitude, and her inherent goodness can and will propel her to do whatever she chooses. I believe that of all daughters; of Blue and Malia and Sasha and Destiny.

There's a section in *Wild at Heart* titled "A Beauty to Rescue." It came to mind as I was reflecting on the job of raising a girl. I hadn't so much as glanced at the book in over a decade, but as I flipped through its pages, now as a husband and father, much of it seemed wildly sexist and criminally dated. While some of the central themes of the book still hold up—the issues that can spring from suppressed desire, the need to overcome fear—others are extreme oversimplifications of the dynamics between men and women. In the author's eyes, every man is called to be Gladiator or Indiana Jones. And every woman is waiting with bated breath for her knight to save her. To swoop by on his white horse, his sword bloody and his face full of dust. As I've noted, this kind of militant masculinity has been around for ages. All of this calls to mind the words of James Dobson, who, in 1980, blasted feminists for challenging "everything traditionally masculine"; for questioning the "time-honored roles of protector and protected." Of course, Dobson is the same man who, in his book *What Wives Wish Their Husbands Knew About Women,* claimed that "men usually like to hunt and fish and hike in the wilderness" and women like to "stay home and wait for them."

It's not hard to see why the trope of the damsel in distress remains one of the most popular literary devices. But it's also tired. Gender-based metaphors often do more harm than good, perpetuating notions of male dominance and female passivity, the woman's need to be *rescued.*

Shout-out to every man and woman priming their sons and daughters to never wait around for permission. If that outlook was ever in fashion, it is no longer. Especially not in my circle, and in circles like mine, where women are not asking for approval to make the life they want for themselves.

Another thing that got me mulling on this was watching my homeboy Nick raise his two young daughters. He's an incredible dad, and he can be tough on his girls, in the best way. He doesn't subscribe to the idea that little girls should be treated like glass houses. No, he launches them high in the sky, teaches them how to spar and knuckle up. He signs them up for any sport or dance class in which they exhibit the least bit of interest. I've seen his girls outsmart and outrun every boy on our block. That's partially a testament to their dad being dope, someone who's intentional in his leadership. A rap dad, through and through.

10

MORE AND MORE A DESIRE GREW IN ME to contest the dominant assumptions about fatherhood—mainly fatherhood in the urban context. I hungered to transmit my perspectives to listening ears. I believed that if we truly were concerned with altering mindsets, we would prove it not only by the way we raise our children but by opening our mouths. Only then could the narrative change. Only then would our stories be told. My friends and I, and young mothers and fathers like us, embodied the promise of a more progressive future. A future that would be formed and cultivated under the influence of our art, music, literature, and the principles by which we lived. I brooded on the possibility of hosting a podcast or pitching a show to networks to see what stuck. There would be compelling guests who shared their stories of hip-hop and parenthood. People would get a view into the personal lives of young parents from angles we've yet to see. Slowly, we would begin to make a dent. My aim was, at least in part, to arrest the eyes and ears of an America that behaved as if we didn't exist. Those who'd called Obama the "food stamp president," the talking heads who believed solely in their own feelings. Those who preferred to tune us out instead of doing the work of overcoming their own ignorance. In the end, I didn't start a podcast, nor did I pitch any show. Whereas I started out energized by the possibilities, in time I grew lukewarm to them, perhaps because I felt inadequate to the task. But I continued writing and interviewing and becoming bloated with ideas that moved me. I knew I had to do my part to help reclaim the narrative of young fathers operating with a different lens.

In 2002, Bill O'Reilly condemned Pepsi for tapping Ludacris to appear in their advertisements. According to O'Reilly then, Ludacris was a rapper who "espouses violence, intoxication, and degrading conduct toward women." A day after the conservative pundit's rant, the soda giant announced that it was dropping the rapper as its spokesperson, apologizing to all who were offended by the initial partnership. O'Reilly praised the company for cutting ties. He'd stated that "Americans should let the merchants of bad taste know that hiring corrupters and incompetents is not acceptable." He said Ludacris was not an artist, but a thug. As it turned out, O'Reilly's plan worked; he got what he wanted.

Following Pepsi's decision, Ludacris spoke out against these assaults on his character, forming a campaign called "It's Got to Be Ludacris." He said in a statement:

"My message represents an ideology and a way of life that is true to me and the new generation to an extent that corporate and political forces can't touch . . . At one time, I helped Pepsi to navigate their product through the inner-city communities that are vital to their sales. Over the past few days I have rethought my approach as to how I do business and retained a team to . . . take the power back for the good of the hip-hop community."

The drama between Ludacris and O'Reilly resurfaced in 2004, when the rapper referenced a sexual harassment lawsuit made against the television host in the track "Number One Spot": "Respected highly, 'Hi, Mr. O'Reilly!' / Hope all is well, kiss the plaintiff and the wifey."

Where O'Reilly used his massive platform to launch his angry attack, Ludacris artfully pointed out that this middle-aged white man had no right to claim any moral agency. In time, people would learn that O'Reilly was culpable of the exact behavior he chose to condemn.

IN A 2011 INTERVIEW with hip-hop personality Sway, Ludacris spoke about a run-in he had with O'Reilly years after the Pepsi incident— at the White House of all places. After O'Reilly approached the rapper and commended him on the great things he'd heard about the Ludacris Foundation, O'Reilly expressed interest in making a financial donation. For all of his bigotry and slander—which would continue for six more years on *The O'Reilly Factor*—he could not deny that the rapper and dedicated father was doing important work through his foundation. He was building a legacy that would outlive him. O'Reilly never mentioned Ludacris on his show again. O'Reilly was fired by Fox News in 2017 following the disclosure of numerous sexual harassment allegations against him.

THE FAULTY LOGIC amplified by many mainstream media outlets—specifically those which aim to cast racial minorities in a negative light—is poison to any democracy. These narratives continuously seek to dehumanize black and Latino men by spreading misinformation and focusing on cases that support their narrow views. These men are often treated unfairly, as if they're all prone to desertion and inevitably doomed to jail or an early grave. But the level of deception packed into the vast majority of these stereotypes is astonishing. And nothing underscores that fact more than how these men are constantly portrayed as absent fathers.

While studies have shown that black and Latino parents are less likely to wed before a child is born, it's foolish to claim that either is prone to neglect. For years, we've been inundated with statistics claiming that black men in particular simply aren't up to the task of fathering. To the contrary, while black and Latino men both remain consistent fathers in their communities, a report by the Centers for Disease Control and Prevention found that black fathers are the most involved with their children daily of any group of fathers.

As Think Progress points out: "Considering the fact that 'black fatherhood' is a phrase that is almost always accompanied by the word 'crisis' in U.S. society, it's understandable that the CDC's results seem innovative. But in reality, the new data builds upon years of research that's concluded that hands-on parenting is similar among dads of all races. There's plenty of scientific evidence to bust this racially-biased myth."

Despite the overwhelming evidence dispelling the mythology

about black fatherhood, this isn't the story you come across on the evening news. Certainly not from political commentators who would rather stick to their same old script. Challenging their audience's understanding of a shifting culture would only disrupt their narrative. In turn, many young black and Latino men internalize society's animosity toward them and accept these indictments as normal. When someone has made up their mind about you, when a group of people have determined to not hear you out or extend any empathy, it makes it hard to care or to seek to convince them of your humanity.

I'm reminded of what Geraldo Rivera said in a Fox News "Race in America" discussion about Lebron James's "I Can't Breathe" T-shirt.

"I wonder to myself," Rivera said, "what if LeBron James had instead worn a shirt, 'Be a better father to your son.' 'Raise your children.'"

Rivera's comments were not only unfounded, they were incredibly tone-deaf considering the simple point the shirt was trying to raise. Eric Garner is the man who was killed by Staten Island police for selling untaxed cigarettes on the street. He was put into a chokehold while lying facedown on the sidewalk. Garner's last words, which he uttered eleven times before losing consciousness, were "I can't breathe." Suffice to say that Rivera's statements did nothing but perpetuate racist ideologies shrouded in arrogance.

PREACHERS OF THIS KIND OF DECEIT are an insult to the most basic tenets of journalism. Their sole wish is to inspire outrage in their disciples; the millions who watch at home waiting for these men and women to tell them whatever their itching ears want to hear. That hip-hop culture is heinous to the core; that black and Latino men and fathers are a drain on society. At the end of the day, it's not the spreading of news and information that gets ratings, but the lens through which that information is presented. Many of these folks, in lacking the ability for self-confrontation, have become enemies of social and cultural progress. Some just don't care to learn; they revel in the good old days, which they conveniently fail to recognize were horrific for millions of others throughout American history. And that's precisely the thing. Many want nothing more than to live unbothered in their communities, never interacting with those who might challenge their toxic biases. Media outlets like Fox News have created the perfect space for dolts to sit idle in their own opinions. The blind leading the blind.

IN 2011, Chicago rapper Common was invited to a poetry event at the White House. The event was organized by Michelle Obama, who was a fan of the artist and his work. But controversy ensued after Fox News labeled Common a "vile rapper" on their website, questioning his past criticisms of former President George W. Bush and law enforcement. The criticism Common received from the likes of Tucker Carlson and Sean Hannity, to name a few, focused on a piece titled "A Letter to the Law," which Common first performed on HBO's *Def Poetry Jam* in 2005. An article written by Neil Munro for the *Daily Caller* compared Common's poetry unfavorably to Emily Dickinson's. "Students, please compare and contrast the two poems," Munro wrote. "You'll get extra credit for counting the death threats. There is no extra credit for identifying spelling errors."

Virtually all of the criticism of "A Letter to the Law" centered on two lines, the first which Munro interpreted as threatening violence against the police: "Them boys chat-chat on how him pop gun / I got the black strap to make the cops run." The second was seen as a threat to former President George W. Bush: "Burn a Bush cos' for peace he no push no button / Killing over oil and grease / No weapons of destruction."

The entire premise of Munro's argument proved to be an exercise in missing the point. He never mentioned—perhaps because Common's piece was above Munro's realm of understanding —that the narrator of the poem ultimately shuns violence and chooses the route of peaceful perseverance. "No time for that, because there's things to be done / Stay true to what I do so the youth dream come."

Prior to this, Common was never viewed as a controversial rapper, but one whose lyrics had long sought to promote positivity and personal and social empowerment. But some don't care to dig deeper for context as it relates to hip-hop and urban art. In his Afterword for the book *The Anthology of Rap*, which also features Chuck D, Common wrote:

"So many of the debates today about rap miss the point. People argue without taking the time to listen to what rap is actually saying. *The Anthology of Rap* explodes the myth that MCs rhyme only about money, cars, and women. Think I'm lying? Open up the book and see for yourself. Even open it at random and you'll find lyrics about love and comic books and bicycles, about God and nature and fatherhood. In other words, about life and the art of living."

ALL OF MY LIFE my curiosity has been irrepressible. Whether it was about the ways of the world, or how I might insert myself into the rhythms of an environment that often felt suffocating. What was it like to be a man and a father who always knew what to do? I tried to inhabit the mind of someone who took to life with total assurance. But there were always questions. This, naturally, led me to books and hip-hop lyrics, the literature and philosophy of my generation. Even as I seemed to be on the periphery of my own life, nothing could stop me from being a seeker. There was always something new to unearth, some new terrain where my mind could wander. It's what led me to investigate the roots of my low-grade depression, to find answers that might provide a clearer grasp of my own father's life and times. But what mattered most was not always the hope of receiving neatly packaged solutions to my queries. Instead, what fueled me often lay in the asking. It was the process of struggling that offered purpose. For me, there was a pleasure in this that drew me to think and to study. Still, it had never before occurred to me that there were those—the Fox News crowd, for example—who had little interest in asking new questions. Many didn't care for entertaining outside worldviews and preferred to stick to what they knew, or what they thought they knew. There wasn't much about "God and nature and fatherhood" and "the art of living" that compelled them to grow in this way.

I was reminded of how skateboarders were often outcasts in the eighties and nineties. Sure, they may have been complicated and rebellious. But often there wasn't much effort made to understand them or to discover what made them tick. They were dismissed as lost, irredeemable; bad news in every sense. And it occurred to me that not all Americans had the defining narratives of the places I grew up. But as we, the young and urban, were now divining the future and working to build a more inclusive tomorrow, others could not fathom the half of it.

Jay-Z: "Legacy, legacy, legacy, legacy."

One spring, I was rummaging through stacks of old shoeboxes, decluttering and organizing. I came across a dozen VHS tapes and dusty issues of *Thrasher*. That magazine, founded in 1981, the year I was born, meant a good deal to me growing up. I'd often tear out the pages and use them to decorate my bedroom walls. Pictures of gods like Ray Barbee, Rodney Mullen, and Tony Hawk, alongside rappers, occupied nearly every inch of space from the floor to the ceiling. Aside from old episodes of *Yo! MTV Raps* and skate classics like *The Search for Animal Chin*—the first skate film to make an attempt at an actual plot—there were other tapes that had long been stashed away. The boys, five and seven at the time, saw my eyes widen as I read off one of the labels which said "Skate or Be Stupid, 1989." It was a home movie filmed with neighborhood friends.

"We have to watch this," said the seven-year-old.

"We have to watch this," echoed his brother.

My sons love it when I tell them stories of my skating adventures, and so a treasure like this one could not be ignored or postponed for viewing at a later date.

AS I MENTIONED EARLIER, skateboarding was for a while the most beautiful form of liberation imaginable. Every kick and push took me further from home and yet connected me more deeply to my environment. When I wasn't watching films and hip-hop videos, I was outside growing braver and adding to my repertoire of tricks. If my parents got into an argument, I would grab my board and shove off with the quickness. It was both ecstasy and sweet rebellion— and it brought me more joy than almost anything for many years of my life. It used to be that skateboarders were perceived as threats, grimy vandals without a single care and their middle fingers permanently outstretched to the law. My "No Code of Conduct" shirt confirmed some of that.

In those days, many cities across the United States were implementing strict skating bans and getting creative in their efforts to stop skaters, from attaching metal prongs to ledges to making pavement surfaces rough. Given how popular the sport has become today, there seems to be less prejudice toward skaters. Yet there is still an underlying rebellion that is at the very heart of the sport. And at the heart of the skater.

AFTER DIGGING OUT THE VCR, I hooked it up and we all three sat to watch, expectant. I wasn't sure what we were about to witness, but one of the first sequences was of eight-year-old me mooning the camera, a stunt the boys naturally found hilarious. Soon enough, though, I was flying through the air, using curbs and speed bumps as launchpads for my courageous and careless acrobatics. The boys were impressed by my skill, shouting for me to rewind parts and captivated by each moment projected on the screen. I felt the sting of pride and pain, and a longing that I'd been suppressing for some time. Seeing them cause a ruckus like this gave me life, and it was, in that instant, my truth.

Serious skateboarding, with all the focus and mental and physical toughness it requires, is a truly singular dance. It shapes you, makes you, calls you to respect your environment in ways no other sport does. I think of veteran skaters like Mike Vallely and Mark Gonzales, their fluid gyrations every bit as poetic and dazzling as a Jay or Nas verse.

"Why don't you do that anymore?" asked the younger after a nimble and seemingly elastic me cleared a two-foot ledge with ease.

"I don't know," I said. It was the best answer I could come up with.

What I wanted to say was that Papi doesn't have time because he has to write and help with dinner and his stupid damn back hurts too much to think about trying.

"Can you teach us how to do it?"

As of this writing, my skateboard is almost exclusively designated for trips to the mailbox, a distance of roughly fifteen yards. In those seconds it takes to head there and back, immense feelings of nostalgia come over me. I miss how it made me feel, how it took my mind off divorce, how the Miami sun warmed me as I practiced my kick-flips and eventually got better and more technical than all the neighborhood squad. I daydream about putting aside anything resembling caution and going mad on the board. But I don't, not full-on anyway. Some days I fear I'm losing something, that rebellion, that edge that's hardwired in the DNA of the skater. See, once you're married and own a home and have children to take to karate and help with homework, it's easy to get too comfortable. You have to make a more conscious effort to keep a healthy dose of rage inside of you; to remember there is always something, some system or broken bureaucracy, to fight like hell. I salute groups like Run the Jewels and poets like Saul Williams who remind me of this.

I often see the teenagers at local parks and am taken aback by how nice they are on the stick. And to add to that, their progress is so easily documented in our digital age. Where the evolution of a skater's ingenuity was once observed mostly through magazines, live appearances, and professionally produced videos, the present offers a multitude of outlets for expression and the immediate gratification of social sharing. What a time to be alive.

It's true that my body is no longer the same machine. In the early two thousands, skateboarding got hard on me. Years of throwing myself down stairs and kissing the ground did their number on my bones, and my psyche. And of course, I've just plain gotten older, a bittersweet reality that comes after us all.

Still, there are more reasons to look forward than backward.

At one point in the home movie, I bring out a garbage can from the garage and place it in the middle of the street. The idea is that we'll ollie over it and see which of us gets the most air. After several botched attempts, the can begins to crack with the weight of our failure. We drag our heads in adolescent, yet very real, frustration. I resolve to give it one last go, because relentlessness is one of any artist's most prized commodities.

The slow buildup gets the boys excited. They wonder aloud if their dad will make it over the mammoth obstacle that's been evading him and his homies for so many tries. Finally, I do, and they go wild there in the dark of our kitchen. I'd persisted, and my biggest reward was—and I didn't know it back then—that my kids would someday see it and beam. That this small win might teach them something about perseverance. The beauty of enduring to the end, of dusting yourself off and doing the damn thing. To my mind, that's a worthy lesson to leave behind should I be gone tomorrow.

FEW ALBUMS MADE ME THINK MORE about the concept of legacy than, you guessed it, Jay-Z's thirteenth studio album, *4:44*. It's a stark and blistering work of memoir, heavy on confession and self-examination. But just four years earlier, *Magna Carta Holy Grail* had folks questioning if Jay had lost his step. It wasn't so much the lyricism and flows on the project that made fans scratch their heads. It was more so that, throughout the album's sixteen tracks, which are chock-full of empty boasts and obscure references, the rapper seemed to be talking *at* people and not *to* them. There was a disconnect that none of his previous work had suffered from.

When word first spread that Jay was releasing something in 2017, it quickly became shrouded in mystery—was *4:44* an album, a film? Like most heads, I was dizzy at the thought of some new Hov, if only a tad skeptical. Especially after Beyoncé's *Lemonade* had left so many unanswered questions regarding his personal indiscretions. When *4:44* finally dropped, I was filled with wonder. How was it that Jay had managed to so fluidly deconstruct everything I'd been wrestling with for the last few years? Though the specifics of our experiences differed greatly, the central ideas dissected on *4:44* had been swimming around my brain for some time. They robbed me of sleep and provoked some of the most intense discussions I'd ever engaged in.

Where No I.D. redefined the possibilities of muddy, sample-based production, Jay reimagined the power of vulnerability in rap without being preachy. Sure, *4:44* is about a lot of things. It's about community, racial politics, the meaning of generational wealth. It's about fatherhood, marriage, and infidelity; it's about coming to grips with the fact that you've been wrong all along. It's the product of the ultimate hustler realizing he's been living by his own selfish accord. And that this living has now damaged the very people he never intended to hurt. More than anything, *4:44* is about a man in need of atonement. A man who mistakenly hauled his baggage into his most cherished relationships. Nas's "Ether," the only worthy attempt at dismantling this legend, was nothing in comparison to the battle Jay was engaged in to save his marriage. He now needed to be rebuilt from the inside out.

Of all the talks I had with friends about some of the themes explored on *4:44*, the most jolting was with Karlie Hustle. Karlie is a former programming director for HOT 97 and a revered music manager and media personality. She's also a wife and mother, a woman of exceptional wit and wisdom. But even a massive Jay-Z fan like Karlie, a firm cultural critic, understands that no one is above reproach. Not even a modern-day icon who'd just become the first rapper ever to be inducted into the Songwriters Hall of Fame. Karlie mainly took issue with the title track on *4:44*, which she viewed as disingenuous. For her, it calls to mind our culture's infantilization of men. "Women are never afforded the same passes as men," she told me. "We're told to adapt to our circumstance and keep it moving, while men are coddled like children."

When Jay hits on bars like "Took for my child to be born, see through a woman's eyes," it only makes Karlie's point. When he offers, "You matured faster than me, I wasn't ready," it bears mentioning that he's addressing a woman eleven years his junior.

IT'S WELL UNDERSTOOD that women generally mature faster than men. A 2013 study published in the academic journal *Cerebral Cortex* offers a scientific explanation. The evidence suggests that the female brain establishes connections and prunes itself faster than the male brain. Which is to say, cognitive development occurs earlier in females, making their brains more efficient. But that's certainly not an excuse to attempt to justify trash behavior (although I've heard men try). Less so when we're talking about basic human consideration as it pertains to love and relationships. As Karlie said, "If it takes for your child to be born for you to see though a woman's eyes, maybe you haven't been listening to women."

I thought a lot about Karlie's agitation with Jay's sentiments. And the more I mulled over the track in question, now having considered it through a woman's perspective, the more I knew she was on the money. Well-meaning men and fathers, good intentions and all, have been at fault for eons. And we who grew up fatherless have, in our way, expected praise for our late epiphanies, our moments of clarity. As if our every realization should be met with a celebratory high five. But that's not life.

RAP, THROUGHOUT ITS HISTORY, has always referenced parenthood in some form. Most often, it was to extol single mothers for their goodness while deadbeat fathers were berated and called out for going ghost. In recent years, as the social media landscape has blown open the avenues of communication, famous rap dads in particular have become increasingly transparent about their lives as family men. This, of course, can prove beneficial in terms of documenting the story. Where years ago there seemed to be endless bars mourning the demise of the father, artists are now using their platform to balance the scales. They're showing themselves to be present and intentional, contending against the fallacies of windbags like Geraldo Rivera. I think of Wiz Khalifa and DJ Khaled. I think of Chance the Rapper. The surge in young men doing the dad thing in public—which in turn inspires everyday fathers everywhere—should, in fact, be celebrated. Not for its own sake, or to give credit to people for doing something "they're supposed to do" as Chris Rock put it. But to confront the mythology. Fact is, our truth must be broadcast even louder so that more diverse voices can echo across the world.

YOU'D BE HARD-PRESSED to find an interview over the last few years where Chance the Rapper doesn't mention fatherhood. His third mixtape, 2016's *Coloring Book,* is not only a spiritual ode to manhood and personal growth, but a gem full of colorful dad raps. For his daughter Kinsley's first year, however, Chance was deliberate about protecting his family's privacy. "My daughter look just like Sia, you can't see her," he rapped on Kanye West's "Ultralight Beam." His daughter wasn't seen on social media until December 31, 2016, when Chance posted a picture of her on Instagram.

In Complex's March 2017 video cover story, Chance sat down with Complex Media's Noah Callahan-Bever, a new father himself. On the digital cover, the then twenty-three-year-old Chance is wearing black overalls over a red shirt, red house slippers, and his signature "3" hat, also red. He's posted on a stool in what looks like a toddler's room, surrounded by toys and trinkets and holding a coffee mug that reads "WORLD'S BEST DAD." It's a fitting visual representation of the rapper's' personal brand: leisurely, measured, and dad to the core.

In the interview, Callahan-Bever asked Chance, straight out the gate, what being the world's best dad means to him. Chance sighed before answering. "I have the world's best dad, currently," he said. "Most of the stuff that he showed me has been his dedication, his time-management, his commitment to being truthful. It's all about what he's instilled in me."

When asked how he's managed to juggle ambition and a hectic schedule with the demands of new fatherhood, Chance showed wisdom beyond his years.

"Balance is something I learned a lot about," he said. "Art just reflects life. It examines life. Anything you create is secondary. It's a reflection of what is actually going on. Existence is the most beautiful thing."

I told myself I could glean from this young man. A lack of balance had been the bane of my life since always. From then on, I rooted for Chancelor Bennett with new vigor.

THE DAYS DRIFTED ON and I kept at it, writing and chasing the visions in my head. The kids were getting older, my wife and I were thriving. One day I called Callahan-Bever, by now a head executive at Def Jam, in a fit of inspiration. I'd long admired his work and was curious how his journey as a father was going.

"I became a father older, at thirty-six," he told me. "I saw the challenges and the sacrifices my father had to make as a young creative. Even though I always felt that I wanted to be a father someday, I knew I had to achieve a level of stability first."

For over an hour we talked about hip-hop and parenthood; we talked politics and his former company Complex's unique position in the culture at large; he told me about his personal ascension from blogger to successful media executive, and some of his most defining career moments.

"I grinded for so many years. I learned that being creative requires a certain level of selfishness. Honestly, the demands sometimes just aren't conducive to parenting. It can be tough to find the head space for projects at times. But I wouldn't change a thing, man. Having a daughter has made me hyper-aware of everything around me, even the stuff I take in. I'm more sensitive to stuff that I was completely numb to as a teenager."

THAT IDEA OF AWARENESS tugged at me; the need to be aware of what I take in and absorb, personally. I don't mean to be moral here, but I remember my friend Cheno—an ex–gang member who now pastors a church—was talking to me about callings. He said everything we do, in some fashion, has a way of affecting our call. Every day, we're either watering that call or we're quenching it. Truth was, I'd made a million futile mistakes over the years. But now I wanted to water the call more. I was now, more than ever, my truest and most secure self. There was a bright and unfamiliar wholeness in me that had been born from living; from my study; from my compulsion to ask questions; from the conversations that had become my daily bread.

"Being a parent has definitely changed my relationship with hip-hop," Callahan-Bever said. "It's reminded me that words matter."

A few days later, my wife took the kids to the library as I had a deadline to meet and needed some space. I was sitting on my balcony, hoping the words would strike me like a hurricane, when I got a message from Ma. A quiet song hung over the damp air, a neighbor plucking at his guitar.

"I think you should talk to your father," Ma wrote, randomly. "I think it will be good," she said. "I reached out to his sister. He wants to talk to you."

For the last several months I'd been asking Ma disjointed questions about my father. More than I ever had before. I was hoping she could help me make meaning of loose ends, questions that lingered in my mind. Why did he jump out of the van that day en route to the Keys? Could she tell me about my cousin who was murdered in Venezuela?

My neighbor kept plucking away. It was the same neighbor I'd seen walking to the pool that morning with his small daughter. He'd recently told me that his longtime girlfriend had ditched him for one of her coworkers, leaving him alone to raise their daughter. He began playing and singing "Dos Gardenias," a bolero by Isolina Carrillo that was later recorded by Buena Vista Social Club.

I WASN'T SURE how I felt about my father's invitation to talk. For starters, it wasn't him who'd initiated the connection after all these years. It was Ma; she'd hoped it might help provide some closure, which she'd assumed I needed but that was far from true. Some days later, Andres, who'd battled a substance abuse addiction for the better part of his twenties, spoke to our father for over two hours. They were practically strangers, since Andres was very small when our folks split. But apparently, their time on the phone had been fruitful. "It was good to hear from him," Andres told us later. "We're really similar and made similar mistakes," he said. "It's a step in a positive direction."

Alejandro didn't seem too interested either, his anger still hot after all this time. There was no animosity in me, though—not like there used to be—just indifference to the proposition. What was there to talk about? I told Ma I'd think about it.

SOME AFTERNOON, I was listening to "Adnis" from *4:44*. The first couplet socked me like a pitch: "Letter to my dad that I never wrote /

Speeches I prepared that I never spoke." Again, Jay had come to me bearing gifts. And in that moment, something was acutely understood. The reason I hesitated at the prospect of speaking to my father now was because part of me felt as though my entire life was a letter to him. Things that remained unsaid were, instead, lived. My failures, as well as my triumphs, were chapters in a living letter I'd been writing to him since I was eight.

"You couldn't kick the habit, I wish you said something / You can't avenge these many sins with your own hands."

My father's mistakes were his alone to live with, this I knew. So while part of me felt sympathy for the man, there was no impulse that spurred me toward any verbal closure. Not immediately. His hands were too short to box with God, and his efforts too feeble to warrant a response from me. But then he started calling. I was in a rush getting the kids ready when he buzzed me on WhatsApp the first time. It was a Saturday, and my hands were tied; I was fastening a car seat and couldn't pick up that instant. He called seven times in a row. Later, I listened to the long message he left, his raspy, aged voice on the verge of nervous. "Qué más mijo," he said. "Es tu papa." He went long about wanting to hear from me. He also said that he'd understand if I wasn't moved to take his call. That I wasn't obligated but that—and he wanted to make this clear—he would love to catch up. The day before I was earnestly considering reaching out. But his drawn-out spiel annoyed the hell out of me, as it suggested he was putting the ball in my court, like some martyr. As if the breaking of years of silence somehow hinged on whether I chose to jump at his calling me out on a whim. I sat with these thoughts for a few nights. Although I knew I was entitled to my disinterest and frustration,

I wondered if there might be a better way. I wondered if I should help him rebuild what we'd lost, or at least try. It had proven beneficial for Andres, so could it also be beneficial for me? And what did that even look like? That I was considering any of this was, for me, proof I was nothing like this man. I decided that if he tried calling again, I'd pick up. My ego puffed up within me.

11

FOR BRIEF STINTS IN THE FALL, a cool breeze floats over Miami's coast, brushes your face and grips your beating heart like a muscle. It's enough to get lost in. Enough to make you forget that, for roughly ten months of the year, the city is a choking hot metropolis that will roast you, day or night. But beneath its menacing and unforgiving exterior—its loud horns and overzealous shop owners hawking discounted luggage—it's a moveable feast. It stays with you. It's more than the limited conceptions of outsiders; more than the posh hotels that line Ocean Drive, the models, and the gleaming vessels of Biscayne Bay. It's deeper than its own obsession with tight bodies and old money. It's also beautiful broken Spanish, life-giving bodegas, and corner prophets announcing that the end is near.

It's in this spirit that I would amble from my office on NE 1st Street, just across from Bayfront Park, to the Cuban café. It's an open window and counter where you walk up and place your order, the sun on your back. There's a plancha for media noches and the ladies serve empanadas, burgers, and the like. Each morning I'd slip in for a fix, a cortadito and two ham croquetas to hold me over for a while. Then I'd retreat to my third-floor office that looked out over the metro servicing the Downtown Miami, Brickell, and Park West neighborhoods. Every few minutes a train would zip past and I'd lift my head up from my work. Occasionally I'd see a face I recognized; a famous friend's mug plastered on a train's skin advertising an upcoming show or festival. I might work for three hours or so—more if it was going well—and feel compelled to take a walk. The walks were clutch. Some days I'd wander for blocks and blocks trying to suss out a piece of writing—picking apart sentences, questioning if my thesis was holding up—hungry and mumbling to myself. Sometimes I just wanted to get out of my head, so I'd cue the Ghostface or Tribe and amble down East Flagler, past the Olympia Theater. Eventually I'd stop someplace to eat. You could only ignore the smells of French, Caribbean, Latin, and Japanese grub spilling out of the kitchens and into the street for so long. If I wasn't with my boys Jaakko and Gerardo—two art directors with whom I shared the space—I might stop at the small cart for Spanish chorizo and munch on the sidewalk. The cart was owned by an older man, short and solid, his serious face time chiseled and sun beaten. Every day he wore a different color guayabera, crisp as a new hundred-dollar bill. One afternoon, as the wind beat against our faces, I lingered around after I'd finished my bite. People were scrambling past in a big important rush; but not us. We exchanged a few pleasantries—the weather, he mentioned his love/hate relationship with the Miami Marlins. I'd been to the man's cart a dozen times before, but somehow we'd never gotten further than the order and the thank-you. We'd been talking some minutes when he asked what I did for a living. I said that I was a writer. He asked me what I was writing, and I told him I was finishing a review of a dystopian sci-fi novel by a Cuban author. His eyes lit up as he revealed to me that he was a poet. That for many years he was heavily involved in the poetry scene in his native Cuba. He told me about his affinity for the work of José Martí, the poet and revolutionary who was committed to the struggle of Cuba's independence from Spain. Martí was also, as the man explained, responsible for what became the island's beloved unofficial anthem, "Guantanamera." He schooled me on the underground poetry scene of his day. He spoke of the literary events he and his friends would hold in Havana, and what they were trying to accomplish against the backdrop of a dictatorship. How they were trying to get free. There was an urgency to their political moment, he told me. And the poetry, he said, was vital to their survival. "Nothing is more important than the work," he said. "Remember that. The work will live on after you're dead and gone."

I thought about the man's words for the rest of the day, and week. About how good work has the potential to carry on well after you expire. How it can caution and inform those that come later. There was a clear parallel for me, as was often the case then, between my work as a father and my work as an artist. Everywhere I turned, something or someone was there to reinforce the question of my personal and professional legacy.

I aspired to join a class of path-breakers—artists and thinkers I'd long revered. People who left their stamp on generations. Luminaries like Sandra Cisneros and disruptors like B-Real and John Leguizamo. Some hip-hop, others not. These were individuals who, though wildly different, broke down walls and did it their way. I'd always longed for some clear and undeniable sense of what I was put here to do. And I felt like I'd finally understood my purpose during our short time in the Midwest, when there was time to breathe and to think. By now I'd been watering this understanding of my duty as a father and writer a good while. "Watering the call" like my friend Cheno had said. And I learned that I was not the only one grappling with similar notions. In certain moments, though, all the weight and conviction bursting within, you could not have convinced me that I was not alone. You could not have convinced me that I was unoriginal in this.

That season in Missouri, away from all that was familiar to me, was the most crucial to my sense of self. I was in a curious position then, because I knew I wouldn't be there very long. I had come for something, and I was determined to stay until I'd found it. It wasn't as extreme as those years overseas—in Honduras, South Africa, Slovakia, Poland, Lithuania, Serbia, Russia, England, and Scotland—but the effects were comparable. On different levels, these forays birthed in me a regard for the benefits of loneliness. The fortitude that loneliness can help birth in you. The combined years away from home helped yield some of the wisdom I hold today. If it were not for them, I cannot imagine what my current state might be.

IN MIAMI, you can be whoever you want to be. You can walk down the street dressed like a luchador, or donning a robe like Jeff Bridges in *The Big Lebowski*, and nobody cares. People have their own problems and agendas. They're busy building the life they want and can't be bothered by your existential crisis. There's green to be made, and the deals aren't going to close themselves. So party hard, by all means. But dick around too long and you'll end up on your face wondering which way is up.

The Magic City seems to always be on the cusp of boiling over. Everyone is in steady pursuit, and reconstruction is happening at a frenetic pace. Highways, towers, restaurants under new ownership. The boom of Coconut Grove, Edgewater, and Midtown has snow-birds flocking in droves. While it may feel open and expansive, it can also get claustrophobic, with cars, stray dogs, and pedestrians all competing for the same space. It's a composite of many moving parts, like any other major metropolitan area. But Miami is a special kind of beast. A rare mix of the laid-back and the utterly mad, a by-product of its international and Caribbean identity. Travelers are fascinated, locals cackle at the memes. To spectators, it'll always be *Scarface*, *Miami Vice*, and *Cocaine Cowboys*. The Mecca of eighties-era organized crime. The shootings that went down at the Dadeland Mall; the riots in Overtown. These are part the story, sure. But considering that as a kid I was closer to South Florida's violent drug wars than most, those waters run deep.

What stirs me most is the focus that powers artists and creative types in a tropical paradise like this one. For better or worse, it moves others to try and measure up, to commit to never being outdone. I think of what Will Smith—purveyor of many wonderful things, including the classic 1998 hit "Miami"—said in a 2007 interview with Tavis Smiley.

Smith: "The only thing that I see that is distinctly different about me is I'm not afraid to die on a treadmill. I will run."

Tavis: "You will not be outworked."

Smith: "I will not be outworked, period. You might have more talent than me, you might be smarter than me, you might be sexier than me. But if we get on the treadmill together, right, there's two things. You're getting off first, or I'm going to die. It's really that simple."

This kind of outlook is something Miami helped nourish in me over the years. In time, I'd committed to not being outworked, to not allowing myself to be silenced, and to telling the stories I wanted to tell the way I wanted to tell them. But it would not have been so, I don't think, if not for what my surroundings had helped produce in me.

I continued to ask questions, stocking my mind with people's unique experiences.

WHEN SHEA SERRANO'S *The Rap Year Book: The Most Important Rap Song from Every Year Since 1979, Discussed, Debated, and Deconstructed* shot up the *New York Times* best-seller list in 2015, I exploded with pride. Not only because Serrano is a Latino writer who was being recognized for his talent—although of course, that—but also because he's a man who's very public about his fatherhood. His three sons get shine on the regular, Serrano's entertaining anecdotes documenting their daily activities in endearing ways. As a father, it can be energizing to watch.

A former teacher, Serrano didn't grow up with brimming aspirations to become a writer. In a way, he stumbled into his current career by accident, scribbling about for extra cash while he and his wife were expecting twins. Little by little, Serrano's work for local papers began to spread, and eventually he was publishing with national outlets and had built a dedicated readership. But it took time. And as he told me over the phone, the work simply doesn't get done if you don't resolve to protect your routine. His years as a schoolteacher and coach had taught him to be intentional with his hours.

"When you're entrusted to provide fifteen meals a day, you just have to be organized," he said. "There's no way to be great at both at the same exact time. You learn how to adjust and make it happen. It reminds me of one of my favorite Lil Wayne lines, where he says, 'Gotta work everyday / Gotta not be cliché.' It's pretty simple, but that's how I approach my work as a writer, and a father, too. Especially a Latino one. We can't be cliché. We got to change people's mindsets about us as men and fathers."

IN *THE ART OF CONVERSATION* Milton Wright posits, "To really become a good conversationalist over the long term it is necessary to acquire the habit of conscientiously stocking your mind with facts and information and then forming opinions on the basis of that knowledge."

Stocking and forming, stocking and forming. That's what I was doing. I was soaking in ideas about the world and about human life until these ideas began to form a sort of unity in my mind. They were a collection of people's personal journeys, those of men and women I respected; the hurts and victories that led them to where they are. People doing their part to reshape and redirect the narrative.

"PEOPLE THINK BLACK AND BROWN FATHERS aren't doing their thing," the producer, record executive, and father of three, 9th Wonder, told me. "They think we're not in our children's lives, but that isn't the case. It's crucial for us to shift these stereotypes and prove them wrong.

"For me, having kids was like being reborn. I became a father when I was twenty. Having a kid right after high school was a challenge, for sure, but I grew into it. It felt important to have someone to take care of, someone to call me Dad. It forced me to grow up quick. These days, more than anything, my son and my daughters help me understand a changing world. They're not attached to the struggle like I was, just like I wasn't familiar with my parents' struggle, who went to school during racial segregation. But it's a new day. Me and my friends are raising kids and at the same time trying to correct the past. We're telling new stories."

Every exchange I had with someone new felt like a public confession, like I was making my hunger known to the masses. My hunger to see our vast community continue to spring up strong around us. And each time, that hunger was reciprocated through tales and sometimes jarring details. Their words hit some string in me, made me realize that, when you got down to it, we all wanted the same thing. We wanted a future that looked more like us, a future that put a premium on our inclusion. We understood that the old world was dying and a new, fresh one would be powered by us and our stories. It was dawning all around us.

AGES AGO, before the kids, and music tours, I found myself back in the classroom. It was summer, and I'd just committed the sin of quitting a gig with no backup. A friend informed me that the K–12 private school where he coached baseball needed teachers for the fall. The proposition seemed odd; I was a college dropout and boasted no credentials. I assumed there was no way anyone would assign me the responsibility of helping mold young minds. I was wrong. As I learned, the faculty and staff were deeply concerned with the school's lack of male teachers, and they desperately wanted to remedy that. My interviews went as well as one could hope. The principal maneuvered around my lack of qualifications and experience by offering me a teacher's aide position. The catch was that it was kindergarten. At first, I was hesitant. Were these kids even toilet trained? Was my temperament suited for dealing with a pack of needy five- and six-year-olds? One thing was certain: I needed a job bad. So after taking into account my options, I accepted the meager pay and set out to do my best Schwarzenegger in *Kindergarten Cop* impersonation. It started out well enough, despite the absence of a subplot going after a notorious drug dealer like Schwarzenegger's John Kimble. Over time, I won favor with the school's leadership, which seemed like a good thing. It wasn't long before I felt completely overextended. The more I proved that I was capable of handling different things, the more I was entrusted with. I'd become more involved with the students than the main teacher, a jaded older woman who was perpetually exhausted. Soon, I was also managing the after-care program. Halfway into the school year, they "promoted" me to in-house substitute. Teachers were always out and they needed someone reliable who could bounce around. This meant I would function as a kind of floater, teaching everything from how to write in cursive to high school biology and AP English. Aside from the fact that I seldom knew what I was doing, it wasn't so bad. Then came the first parent-teacher conference. I was asked to lead it because the main teacher had gotten hit with the flu. The tables had turned and now I found myself on the other side, sitting across from the parents of a hyperactive first grader who was terrorizing his classmates. Around this time, I had developed the habit of scribbling on my hands. Lyrics, illustrations, notes to self. I'd jot them on my palm in black ink and shoot them a glance from time to time. Sometimes the smaller kids would ask about them and I'd read the words aloud or explain the doodle. "They're reminders," I'd tell them. But they were more than that. They were kernels that got at some bit of truth I wanted to keep top of mind. The boy's parents pointed out in the conference that their son had started doing the same. Instead of stopping at his hand, he wrote and drew on everything; his sister, the bathroom walls, on the seats of the family car. "Mr. Vidal does it," the boy would say when he was reprimanded at home. His mother believed adamantly that I was to blame, and I sat back and took it. I apologized for their son's actions, and for the remainder of my year at the school, I stopped making an art project of my hands. I'd done it for the same reason some people cover their bodies with tattoos: to tell myself the stories I resolved never to forget.

Sometime before this, some friends and I had got it into our minds to go protesting. More accurately, we wanted to make a mockery of the presidential elections. This was after the 2000 campaign, when Al Gore was said to have lost the electoral vote to George W. Bush. Folks were heated and our state of Florida was considered the country's inept stepchild.

Before we left the house, we figured it might be appropriate to fashion some signs, as any impassioned activists would do. We sat for close to an hour, wound up, staring back and forth at one another, uncertain of what to broadcast on our neon poster boards. Whatever it was, it had to pack a punch. It had to detail our frustration and make known our tenacity, our demand to see change. Finally, someone yelled, "How about 'Bring back Arsenio'?" A nod, of course, to the famed late-night talk show host whose program was a landmark in the early 1990s.

WE HAD BIG LAUGHS, impressed with our genius and anxious to see how our message would translate to the public and to the governing officials of our great democracy. Would they entertain our request or dismiss us as the pseudo freedom fighters we were? Either way, the voice of the people would be heard, we said in our defense. We thought to make one more sign, and after some moments of deliberation, went with "Blame it on John Rocker," the Georgia pitcher notorious for curveballs and hateful tirades. "Don't forget the video camera," I barked.

We packed into the Dodge and headed for West Palm Beach, fifty miles north of us, where the newspeople were. During the drive we mused and planned and conducted interviews with one another about how our protests would be felt.

Upon arrival, we found ourselves in the center of an uprising, a real-life protest. We considered abandoning the idea altogether, but reconsidered once we saw a few people actually snicker at our bravery. Conservatives and liberals lined the streets like trees. A group of police officers laughed to themselves as we ambled past with our bubble letter proclamations. At this point, getting arrested almost sounded novel, charming, like a story you tell your grandchildren by a fire. As we approached the news cameras, all attention shifted our way, just as we'd hoped it would but secretly did not. Many of the onlookers were confused. Were we serious? Others stood militantly as they gawked at us with eyes of disgust, cussing and burning red as cigarette tips. Fear settled in. Please God, don't let me get stole in the mouth, I thought. I told myself not to punk out, for the sake of the story. Then, in a moment of blind courage, I walked directly behind the reporter, "Bring Back Arsenio" sign in grasp, as she articulated the night's events to the families at home. An elderly man cursed my children as he wielded his sign reading, "We demand a recount."

The night was strangely exhilarating. Aside from the angry rebukes, fun was had by all. But the drive home was, for me, thick with reflection. City lights beamed and soared above us, much like the resolve of the protesters. I wondered at their passion, questioning my own and asking if I'd ever be willing to fight for something I believed in. The aim had been to make a mockery of the whole scene. The scolding we received, in a way, suggested the accomplishment of our objective. As if on cue, a greater truth presented itself in my mind almost immediately. We were apathy personified, three clowns passionate about nothing.

I was thoroughly shaken by how useless I'd felt on that fall night in November of 2000. Less than a year later, I was aboard a plane, embarking on that first trip to Central America. Invigorated by the thought of doing something that might prove significant. What followed was the making of a life; international travels, countless blunders, lessons in selflessness, marriage, and the simple dreams of fatherhood.

I'M SITTING IN A COFFEE SHOP in West Midtown Atlanta. A little girl about seven years old sways in her Sunday dress at a nearby table. In front of her is a thin, slightly worn coloring book decorated with owls, butterflies, and koi fish. She surveys the room—the people, the industrial ceilings, and the murals on the walls—waiting for inspiration to strike. Then she carefully applies her pinks and blues to her masterpiece-in-progress. Her tongue pokes slightly out of the side of her mouth, a gesture reserved for tasks as severe as this one. She's alone, but not really. At the table behind her are her parents, having a private conversation. I sense the tension in their body language, and in their mindfulness to shield the girl from their words. I can't help but learn that this is a relationship that is ending. A relationship, possibly a marriage, I can't be sure, of over ten years. Nothing unusual there. At the risk of sounding overly sentimental, I'll say that exchanges like this one, between two adults, cause me grief. Despite this, I conclude they'll all be better off, since myriad of research shows that the children of broken-up parents generally manage fine. Still, I mourn the death of a union. I wonder what the artist next to me, who's doing her best to shade perfectly inside the lines, will make of the next few years of her life. How she'll process the meaning of the world and her role in it. I want to believe that, in time, something will satisfy her hunger to be fully alive, like hip-hop did for me. But I can't know for certain.

I come here two or three times a week these days, to work or to be still. I sit in the back by the large window that faces the traffic, faces the city my family and I now call home. Atlanta is a city of transplants. More than half of the adult population has come from elsewhere, from hectic boroughs and small towns. It's a city of renewed artistic vision, where streets double as galleries, and the entertainment industry has flocked to take advantage of Georgia's tax credits.

I'd always been charmed by the idea of Atlanta, admiring it from a distance, through Outkast and Goodie Mob records. Thanks to their lyrics, I'd memorized places and the names of streets—East Point, College Park, Decatur, Headland and Delowe. When I thought of Atlanta, I'd picture the late Lisa "Left Eye" Lopes torching her boyfriend, NFL wide receiver Andre Rison's $2 million estate in Alpharetta. I'd think of the 1960s, when Atlanta was at the heart of the Civil Rights Movement. Like other regions in the American South, its history is imbued with politics and deep racial tensions. Now it is, among other things, hip-hop's center for gravity. The trap sound it birthed has become more influential than the sound of any other place on the map. It's what New York and Los Angeles were to rap in the 1990s.

This morning, a blue sky covers the city like a blanket. Blue as the bluest eye. I'm here, clutching my life in my mind. I've seen much destruction; I've seen beauty. Like most others, my mind has processed heartache and loss, joy. It's a strange thing to look back upon your life and the many turns that brought you to the present. I think of the Colombia my parents narrowly escaped; I think of the prison system I managed to dodge. I've cobbled together a million and one stories trying to make out the unknowable shape of the future; what secrets the sun and moon might hold in their blinding glare. I think of all the ways I've been wrong. At some point it got in my mind that success was my end-all. That my worth would be found only in what I gathered for myself. I know now that this was a fallacy, a conclusion I'd come to solely out of fear; out of the need to prove that I was, as it were, a man. I saw in time that the meaning of my life did not hinge on any of that, but on what I might give, and how I might invest in others. I'm not talking about hope, though, not exactly. When I say invest, I mean fight. I mean that, while the world can often seem harsh and irredeemable, there is still very much worth fighting for.

The reason I'm here this bright morning, in the coffee shop, is that I'm waiting for a call from Tomás. Last I heard, he had three seeds and was making major moves in Manhattan. After several weeks of trying to track him down with no luck, I finally got his numbers from a mutual acquaintance. We traded a few messages on WhatsApp and set aside time to catch up, to fill each other in on what the years had made of us as men. How the light of life had at last descended upon us after what felt like an impenetrable darkness. *I can't believe it's been so long,* he wrote. From our brief text correspondence, I gathered that he was the man and father I always knew he would someday become.

They say you shouldn't meet your heroes, and I understand why.

I think I understood it a long time ago. What I didn't expect was that my true and lasting heroes would end up being my lifelong comrades and crew, those whom I'd seen crush fear and shift the wind. The children of immigrants, the fatherless, those who were once cast aside for being unruly and good-for-nothing. Those who scrawled rap lyrics in their textbooks because the counterculture had helped form and inform their world more than anything else. I admire so many of the fathers I know. Like them, I fantasize about being the greatest one there is. It's a fantasy fathers understand. It's a beautiful thing what we're doing if you stop and think about it. How we're helping build the earth, populating it with arrows. But today I liken fatherhood, not so much to being some mighty warrior, but to being an artist. Both are creators, and making myself available in the service of both callings has become my life's work. I've come to know that great artists, like great parents, can be the best mirrors for us all.

In *Walking on Water*, Madeleine L'Engle writes, "The artist must be obedient to the work, whether it be a symphony, a painting, or a story for a small child. I believe that each work of art, whether it is a work of great genius, or something very small, comes to the artist and says 'Here I am. Enflesh me. Give birth to me.'"

All art, like fatherhood, is incarnational; it brings life. It breathes into a void, makes a life out of purely nothing.

I think of what the rapper Rapsody once told me. She said, "Hip-hop started as a voice for the people, by the people. For a long time, it's provided a kind of solidarity, a way to tell our truth and to bring a message that only the people can decode." I like that picture, too. Because even though some will try to silence that which they don't understand, we'll still be here, telling the stories that matter to those willing to listen and decode. It is only our stories that have the capacity to untwist and provoke dull minds.

My phone rings. As I answer, I hear a slew of kids screaming in the background. My old friend takes a moment and calmly, skill-fully, settles them down. It's my boy on the phone, he tells them. Chill. In an instant, my mind is stripped dry as a bone. All I want to do is listen to his story, which is also the story of us.

Epilogue

THERE WERE MANY SETBACKS ALONG THE WAY that threatened the completion of this book. While a bulk of my thinking life has been spent kicking around much of what is contained here, the evolving dilemmas of the world, and of my own personal world, delayed its making. But I'm thankful for what these delays produced in me. Books shouldn't be written until they're good and ready.

The social and political climate in which we find ourselves is one of selective listening. For this reason, at least to my mind, there has been no better time to have these conversations. Especially with the influence of hip-hop being what it is now. For far too long, the dialogue concerning who will lead coming generations into the future has been one-sided. But hip-hop heads, in their collective genius, have never been the type to conform.

The world learned recently that, for the first time since Nielsen started measuring music consumption in the United States, hip-hop is, by far, the top musical genre. And even though many of us knew its force—and the influence of the culture as a whole—was already the most powerful, the publicizing of this data is worth noting.

There's more: according to another study by researchers in Britain, hip-hop caused the biggest evolution in American pop music over the last half century. The study involved a digital analysis of chord patterns and tonal shifts in over 17,000 songs on the U.S. pop charts between 1960 and 2010. "Hip-hop is the single greatest revolution in the U.S. pop charts by far," said Armand M. Leroi, professor of Evolutionary Developmental Biology at Imperial College London, a coauthor of the study. "That surprised me. Being a victim of boomer ideology, I would have said it was 1964." Of course the music is only part of the thing. Hip-hop culture's ability to impact societies at such a high level is unparalleled, making it the most important youth movement in all the world. A youth movement that is led by the young as well as many seasoned veterans, those whose voices continue to matter after decades. This, naturally, directly correlates to the changing face of fatherhood in America and the world. As the movement grows, its practitioners age. These are the ones helping to shape—through their testimony, experience, and wisdom—a more considerate future for all. A future that reflects the power of representation.

People want to believe that the arc of the moral universe bends toward justice; toward freedom and fairness. But not until people begin to regard the stories, and the bodies, of those whom they perceive as other, will there be any genuine transformation. Minorities across America will continue to find themselves subjected to a peculiar violence, a violence perpetuated by those who wish with all their might to reign over the world. What becomes apparent

JUAN VIDAL

is this: the only way for people to grow in empathy toward their neighbor is to listen. To put in the work; to be willing to have their hearts and minds broken and opened. If so many of us could shed, for example, the harmful patriarchal views that were a product of our upbringing, I must believe others can discard their own twisted inheritances. Until then, we'll keep the cypher going; and that cypher is 360 degrees of Knowledge, Wisdom, and Understanding.

Salute to the rap moms and dads. Salute to the real.

Acknowledgments

FIRST, GRATITUDE TO THE FAMILY. To Rheagan, my heart. To my main squad, Elijah, Jonas, Elianna Lucia, and Lucas. You're everything.

Thank you to my agent, Monika Woods, who saw the vision and changed my life. To my editor, Todd Hunter, for his wisdom and steady hand. You're a real one, sir. One time for copy editor Rick Willett for being magic. To Wendolyne Sabrozo, Alysha Bullock, and the rest of the team at Atria Books for their hard work and trust.

To all the editors I've worked with, especially Petra Mayer, who has always pushed me and never let me get off easy. You're a gem.

To my crew: Konata, Amanda, Gabe, you already know. We've been through it all, and I'm in yall's corner to the death. Danny, Luis, and Jacob. Us for life. Miri and Carson, two superwomen. Kev and Jon, Stacey and Jess. To the rest of the brotherhood, Cheno, Marty, Fern, Rey King. I'd go to war for ya'll, anytime, anyplace. Nick and Lex, thanks for always holding us down.

Also: Alex Medina, Matthew Warren, Joe Gonzalez, Saul Williams, Lecrae, Trip, Jordan Sparrow, Prop, Wes Pendleton.

Thank you to the amazing and gracious folks who came through on this book: RZA, Adisa Banjoko, 9th Wonder, Phonte Coleman, Noah Callahan-Bever, Karlie Hustle, Shea Serrano, Rapsody, and Combat Jack (RIP).

Love to my hermanos Alejandro, Andres, and Joey.

Ma, thank you for being you. I hope I've made you proud. Te adoro.

To Joe, for your love and leadership.

My tíos Carlos and Nicolas for years of inspiration and incredible stories.

My extended fam has been a rock for years: Thank you to Jeff and Melody, Aaron and Moriah, Gentry.

And Thank YOU.

Track List

Eric B. & Rakim, "Don't Sweat the Technique"
A Tribe Called Quest, "Keeping It Moving"
Black Moon, "I Got Cha Opin"
Public Enemy, "Terminator X to the Edge of Panic"
Public Enemy, "Bring the Noise"
Public Enemy, "She Watch Channel Zero?!"
XV, "Pictures on My Wall"
Public Enemy, "Public Enemy No. 1"
Jay-Z, "Blue Magic"
Scarface, "Crack"
Lupe Fiasco, "Kick Push"
Lupe Fiasco, "Hurt Me Soul"
Wu-Tang Clan, "C.R.E.A.M."
Cypress Hill, "I Wanna Get High"
Earl Sweatshirt, "Chum"
The Notorious B.I.G, "One More Chance"
Method Man, "Tical"
Pink Floyd, "Young Lust"

Pink Floyd , "Is There Anybody Out There?"

Black Star, "Respiration"

Ghostface Killah, "Winter Warz"

Slum Village, "Fall in Love"

Craig Mack, "Flava In Ya Ear" (Remix)

Drake, "From Time"

Tupac, "So Many Tears"

Sisqó, "Thong Song"

Jeru the Damaja, "Come Clean"

Talib Kweli, "Joy"

Common, "The Food"

Chance The Rapper, "Blessings"

Raekwon, "Incarcerated Scarfaces"

Raekwon, "Guillotine (Swordz)"

Little Brother, "Away from Me"

Jay-Z, "Glory"

Common, "Retrospect for Life"

Jay-Z, "Dirt Off Your Shoulder"

Kendrick Lamar, "How Much a Dollar Cost"

Public Enemy, "Fight the Power"

Nas, "Daughters"

Ludacris, "Number One Spot"

Nas, "Ether"

Jay-Z, "4:44"

Kanye West, "Ultralight Beam"

Buena Vista Social Club, "Dos Gardenias"

Jay-Z, "Adnis"

José Martí, "Guantanamera"

Will Smith, "Miami"

Lil Wayne, "Dr. Carter"